CONDUCTING INDIVIDUALIZED EDUCATION PROGRAM MEETINGS THAT WITHSTAND DUE PROCESS

ABOUT THE AUTHOR

James N. Hollis is a practicing clinical psychologist living in San Antonio, Texas. He earned his M.A. in psychology and his Ph.D. in special education from the University of Texas. He completed formal post-doctoral training in clinical psychology, including a residency in the child and adolescent service of the clinical psychology training program at the University of Texas Health Sciences Center in San Antonio. Dr. Hollis is listed in the National Register of Health Service Providers in Psychology and holds a specialty license in school psychology. Dr. Hollis has held adjunct faculty positions at the University of Texas, Trinity University, and the University of Texas Health Sciences Center in San Antonio. Dr. Hollis also earned a law degree from the University of Texas Law School, where he served on the Board of Editors of the *Texas Law Review*. Following clerkships in federal district and appellate courts, he worked as an associate attorney with a prominent Texas school law firm practicing in the areas of civil rights and special education litigation. He has worked as a consultant primarily assisting attorneys, public school districts, and parents in special education matters. His professional interests lie in the areas of childhood emotional disturbance and behavior disorders, special education law, mental health law, and children's rights.

CONDUCTING INDIVIDUALIZED EDUCATION PROGRAM MEETINGS THAT WITHSTAND DUE PROCESS

The Informal Evidentiary Proceeding

By

JAMES N. HOLLIS, J.D., PH.D.

CHARLES C THOMAS • PUBLISHER, LTD.

Springfield • Illinois • U.S.A.

Published and Distributed Throughout the World by

CHARLES C THOMAS • PUBLISHER, LTD.
2600 South First Street
Springfield, Illinois 62794-9265

© *1998 by* CHARLES C THOMAS • PUBLISHER, LTD.
ISBN 0-398-06846-1 (cloth)
ISBN 0-398-06847-x (paper)

Library of Congress Catalog Card Number: 97-32856

With THOMAS BOOKS *careful attention is given to all details of manufacturing and design. It is the Publisher's desire to present books that are satisfactory as to their physical qualities and artistic possibilities and appropriate for their particular use.* THOMAS BOOKS *will be true to those laws of quality that assure a good name and good will.*

Printed in the United States of America
DR VB-R-3

Library of Congress Cataloging in Publication Data
Hollis, James N.
    Conducting individualized education program meetings
that withstand due process : the informal evidentiary proceeding / by James N. Hollis.
        p.   cm.
    Includes index.
    ISBN 0-398-06846-1. -- ISBN 0-398-06847-x (pbk.)
    1. Handicapped children--Education--United States.
2. Individualized instruction--United States. 3. Meetings--
United States--Planning. 4. Home and school--United
States. I. Title.
LC4031.H636   1998
371.9'0973--dc21   97-32856
                                                              CIP

PREFACE

The IEP team meeting is the heart of IDEA's procedural safeguards for children with disabilities. IDEA's procedures are the key to its substantive success. This book is written to help parents, school administrators, teachers, and assessment professionals meet basic requirements of conducting an IEP team meeting in a way that produces defensible IEP decisions in a litigious environment. In today's environment, parents and professionals should assume the decisions they make as IEP team members likely will be scrutinized and second-guessed later on by an outside expert, lawyer, or judge. This implies information relied upon to make IEP decisions must be comprehensive, relevant, and based on verifiable fact and qualified opinion. Solid, well-supported IEP decisions discourage litigation, if the IEP team can show that it thoroughly considered current assessment and expert opinion, clarified each dispute or area of concern among team members, and documented the evidence and reasoning supporting the team's resolution of each issue in the IEP.

If you run IEP meetings, or participate actively as a parent, this book should help you learn to treat the IEP team meeting as an evidentiary proceeding, not unlike an informal hearing, where the IEP team's decisions may be appealed, and judged, according to certain standards. These standards include: whether only relevant and competent data, i.e., evidence, was considered; whether the team gave proper weight to each piece of evidence; whether the team recessed to obtain more evidence if the record was lacking on an essential element needed for decision; whether the team gave all persons with relevant, competent evidence an opportunity to be heard; whether the team made logical, reasonable inferences to reach conclusions from the evidence; and whether the team developed strategies logically related to those conclusions. The book thus presents an approach to putting data before the IEP team, structuring deliberations, and documenting decisions, to make it more likely that participants confront and use relevant information in an orderly fashion to make certain common types of IEP decisions.

CONTENTS

CONDUCTING INDIVIDUALIZED EDUCATION PROGRAM MEETINGS THAT WITHSTAND DUE PROCESS

Chapter 1

INTRODUCTION

I. GOALS, OBJECTIVES, AND LIMITATIONS OF THE BOOK

The purpose of this book is to orient parents, school administrators, teachers, and assessment professionals to the basic requirements of conducting an IEP team meeting in a way that produces careful, defensible IEP decisions. Parents and school professionals no longer can sit around the table comfortably assuming that their decisions will never be the subject of a special education due process hearing, or some other form of administrative or judicial review. Rather, complaints and hearings are so prevalent today that we should all assume the decisions we make as members of an IEP team will, more likely than not, be scrutinized and second-guessed at some future date by a lawyer, an outside "expert," or an administrative or district court judge. None of the usual members of an IEP team are trained or otherwise disposed to run the IEP meeting like a courtroom proceeding, where the information used to make decisions has to be comprehensive, relevant, and based on verifiable fact and qualified expert opinion. But in today's litigious world of special education, teachers, administrators, assessment personnel, and parents could benefit from approaching IEP team meetings in just this way, with one eye focused on making a record for appeal, in order to get the most from IDEA's procedural safeguards.

The IEP team meeting is the heart of IDEA's procedural safeguards. The Supreme Court in *Board of Education v. Rowley* reminds us that IDEA's procedures are seen as the key to its substantive success. That is, if the IEP team uses correct procedures, then more often than not the IEP team will make the best decision in the interest of the child. Those who have litigated special education due process hearings, prepared for hearing, or struggled through hearing as a witness know this: mediation or settlement, based on a mutually agreed-upon resolution, usually produces a more satisfactory outcome for the child than going to trial. Settling differences at an IEP team meeting is even better. But all participants have to approach IEP team meetings with diligence and genuine sensitivity to all members' concerns. This promotes careful consideration of all relevant data and makes use of each member's input. Approaching the IEP process in the right spirit often allows parties to avoid a hearing request altogether, before conflict-resolution strategies are forced on team members by outside authorities. Most disagreements can be resolved without recourse to a due process hearing. But if a hearing is necessary, we believe it can proceed to resolution with a minimum of cost and consternation if the IEP team already has done a proper job of creating a record that (1) demonstrates awareness of current assessment and expert opinion, (2) clarifies specific disputes or areas of concern, and (3) documents the evidence and reasoning behind the resolution of each issue feeding into the IEP itself.

If you run IEP meetings or participate actively as a parent, this book should help you to rethink your task. The book may convince you to begin treating the IEP team meeting as an evidentiary proceeding, not unlike a formal or informal hearing, where the IEP team's decisions may be judged on: (1) whether the proper data, i.e., evidence; was put in front of the team; (2) whether the team gave proper consideration and "weight" to each piece of evidence in the event of conflicting trends; (3) whether the team recessed to obtain more evidence if the record was lacking on an essential requisite for decision; (4) whether the team gave all persons with relevant information an opportunity to speak and/or to present records; (5) whether the team made, and documented, logical and reasonable inferences to reach conclusions from the "evidence," and (6) whether the team developed objectives and strategies logically related to those conclusions. The book may or should cause the IEP team to do several things differently:

- organizing and evaluating the "evidence" that needs to be put before the IEP team;
- making strategic decisions concerning the proper participants in the IEP team meeting and their respective roles;
- ensuring that all relevant information is put before the team;
- anticipating issues that may arise during the meeting but should be channeled to other decision-makers besides the IEP team;
- considering parent input more carefully;

- and most important, reexamining what information is likely
  to be important for each type of decision the IEP team makes.

We know that you know there are no quick, easy formulas for making good decisions, where the issues are as complex as the issues IEP teams face every day. The complexity of these decisions surely cannot be captured by any formula or checklist, though many special educators attempt to standardize the process with checklists for various purposes. We work in a field where good-faith disputes abound concerning appropriate classification, causation, and remediation. But IDEA codifies the hope that by relying on current information, conducting appropriate timely assessment, inviting the key stakeholders to contribute, and providing avenues of appeal, the resulting decisions will deliver appropriate education for children. This book is intended to help you improve the decision-making process of your IEP teams so that the resulting IEP is defensible, that is, it flows reasonably from the best evaluative information available to the decision makers, is capable of passing the "stranger" test, and most importantly delivers a program that benefits the child in meaningful ways.

II. FORMAT AND STRUCTURE OF THE BOOK: HOW TO USE IT

The book presents an approach to putting data before the IEP team, structuring deliberations, and documenting decisions, to make it more likely that participants confront and use relevant information in an orderly fashion. The book proceeds by showing how to apply this approach to common types of decisions that IEP teams must make. The types of decisions addressed in the book are:

1. Discipline
2. Inclusion/LRE
3. Specific goals and objectives
4. Behavior intervention/management plans
5. Related services
6. Special education: methodology
7. Medical and health care services
8. Assistive technology
9. Reimbursement of private services and residential placement

The book is written in an easy-to-use format to help the reader quickly achieve an overview for planning the meeting, with greater detail within the specific sections to give the reader suggestions on how best to address that particular area and what specific tasks may need to be scheduled before the IEP team meeting. Following a discussion of our underlying assumptions regarding issues that are not specifically addressed by the model, each chapter will address one of these specific types of IEP decisions.

III. ASSUMPTIONS: THINGS THAT TAKE PLACE BEFORE THE IEP MEETING

Compliance with Procedures

The book assumes that the school district and the parent have followed IDEA's basic procedural requirements. For the school district's part, we assume a school representative has done the following: (1) given the parents appropriate and timely notice of the IEP team meeting, including the issues to be discussed and the names, or at least the positions, of the persons who will attend the meeting on behalf of the school district; (2) completed a current comprehensive individual assessment report and such additional assessments as may be needed to address changed circumstances; (3) made necessary administrative arrangements for key school district participants to attend the child's special education teacher; the child's general education teacher; an assessment professional if appropriate; and an administrator who can address placement alternatives, resolve discipline issues, and assure that the school district will deliver the services ultimately included in the IEP; (4) provided parents with notice of rights and procedural safeguards; and (5) assured that all school staff have accurate knowledge of parent rights and appropriate procedures. For the parent's part, we assume that you have done the following: (1) read and understood the essentials of the current IEP; (2) received and understood an explanation of the child's current assessment; (3) received and understood an explanation of all IDEA procedural rights; (4) if possible, advised the school district of whom you intend to bring with you to the IEP team meeting; and (5) to the extent possible, notified school staff in advance of any disagreement you have regarding actions the school has proposed.

Familiarity with Procedural Options

This book assumes that a school representative will attend the IEP meeting who has a working knowledge of the extensive procedural rights and safeguards available both to parents and to the school district in the event of a dispute over the IEP. Preferably a friend or advocate will be available also to assist the parent, if necessary, in case of a dispute. For example, someone on the team should know when and how to ask for a recess of the meeting, or request further assessment data, if necessary. The former IDEA regulations contemplated that the IEP team would recess when it becomes apparent that further assessment or other information is needed. The team may recess for as long as the team finds it appropriate to recess. If the duration of the recess is lengthy, however, it may be necessary for the team to establish agreed-upon interim measures in undecided areas to minimize any interruption of services.

The team also should recess at the point the team members feel that deliberations have bogged down or become irrational, such that any new input would be helpful. In addition to obtaining further assessment or reviewing additional information, a recess also gives the school representative and the parent and his or her representatives an opportunity to regroup, obtain additional input, rethink opinions, and return to the deliberations from a fresh perspective. If the team must recess because of a strong disagreement between the parent and the school's representatives, and the process has reached the point that the team needs no further assessment, a recess may be appropriate to consider whether to pursue some form of alternative dispute resolution, before one side or the other requests a due process hearing. The parent should be in the position of feeling confident about their understanding of all IDEA procedural rights and options, including mediation which states now must make available if parties desire it.

The school's representatives should always discuss with the parent all available options for resolving conflict short of a due process hearing, including having the parent bring nonlawyer advocate representatives to the IEP meeting, employing a neutral case manager or outside expert to assist with decision making and conflict resolution, and requesting assistance from an impartial mediator appointed by the state or contracted from another source. It may even be productive for both the parent and the school to bring legal counsel to the meeting, if counsel are knowl-

edgeable and experienced with special education legal and substantive issues. Experienced counsel are not just for litigation but can also help resolve disputes. While the expense is high, reliance on counsel lacking special education background may do more harm than good.

Some parents and school representatives are not aware that federal
law does not require the use of attorneys in special education due process hearings. Many hearings proceed with the parents representing
themselves and their child or having a lay advocate assist presentation
of the parent's case. Similarly, the school may elect to have an administrator or other school professional present the school's side of the case
to the special education hearing officer. This approach may be desir-
able when the only real disputes concern factual matters ("what really
happened") or possibly expert opinions ("what will work and what
won't") and the parties have no real dispute about what the law is or
how the law should apply once the facts are decided. Conducting a
hearing in this manner saves the money that parents and the school
otherwise would pay lawyers and may avoid some of the acrimony that
a lawyer-driven adversary proceeding sometimes engenders or aggra-
vates. By contrast, if the dispute involves novel or difficult issues of law,
or the application of law to fact, and the parties already are thinking
about appeal to district court in the event of a loss at hearing, then proceeding without counsel at the hearing stage would be a mistake. Similarly, if one side has an attorney, generally the other side should also.

In anticipating legal proceedings where "facts" must be proven by evidence, schools and parents must remember that the ideal practice is to
have more than one source of evidence to confirm the existence of any
alleged fact. Teacher statements, for example, are certainly good, competent evidence, but they are more reliable if backed up by contemporaneous
records such as work that the child herself has completed that illustrates the
teacher's statements about learning characteristics and/or progress. The
same holds true for statements of any potential witness and any person
bringing information or proposals for the IEP team's consideration.

Preparation for Meeting

Beyond these basics, we also tend to assume that both the parent and a representative from the school district an administrator, assessment professional, or special education supervisor will have finished other tasks to prepare for a meeting. IEP team members should be able to anticipate, at least in general terms, what topics other participants will bring up for discussion at the meeting, particularly any anticipated differences of opinion or areas of disagreement. Other key tasks include: (1) reviewing carefully the current assessment and its recommendations before the IEP team meeting; (2) conferring in person with, or obtaining written notes or a checklist from, each of the child's teachers regarding the student's strengths, problem areas in their class, including behavior problems and/or emotional symptoms, and progress on the essential elements of the teacher's grade and subject (for general education classes) as well as progress on IEP objectives set at the last IEP team meeting; (3) updating the comprehensive individual assessment and/or statement of present competencies in any area related to the student's difficulty, where the IEP has convened to consider the student's failure to progress or regression; and (4) updating the comprehensive individual assessment in areas that might be related to the student's behavior, where the IEP team convenes to consider whether a behavioral incident was or was not a manifestation of the student's disability or an inappropriate placement. Since parents have access to the child's teacher and the child's educational records, this book assumes that the parent has obtained and reviewed relevant information from the school district relating to the child's assessment and progress and, if necessary, has obtained assistance to clarify questions about the meaning or interpretation of that data.

Requesting a Meeting: When and Why

It will be assumed that the school district and the parent understand when and why it may be necessary to request an IEP team meeting, what problems the IEP team has the authority to address, and what issues are best pursued through a different administrative process. Federal law requires the IEP team to meet at least once a year, but contemplates that the team also may convene more frequently any-time it may be necessary to consider (1) the anticipated needs of the child, (2) the results of any assessment or evaluation, (3) the child's lack of expected progress, (4) new information provided by the parents, and (5) the relationship between the child's disability or placement and behaviors that trigger certain disciplinary consequences. These critical circumstances should dictate convening an IEP team meeting. We assume parents and educators are alert to such circumstances, realizing that the IEP team has an essential and continuous responsibility to address changes in the child's status and needs. This means convening an IEP team promptly when necessary and not postponing pressing issues until the annual review.

Public schools have administrative and other legal procedures for handling most non IEP decisions that affect the child with a disability, and those procedures should be used, instead of the IEP meeting, to resolve issues that do not directly concern the child's IEP. Complaints of misconduct against teachers or administrators, for example, are normally not appropriate for the IEP team to address. The IEP team is not the appropriate public school entity authorized to put negative reference letters in a school employee's personnel file, nor to demote or discharge school employees. State regulations and local school policies have other procedures for parties to bring personnel complaints to the school board or other entity with legal responsibility for school governance. Complaints about participation of students with disabilities in extracurricular activities ordinarily will not raise issues for the IEP team but rather are appropriate for a grievance to the school board, to another entity that regulates athletics participation, or to the Office of Civil Rights under Section 504 of the Rehabilitation Act.

In contrast, nothing that directly impacts the effectiveness of a disabled child's educational program can be precluded from consideration by the IEP team, so long as the issue can be addressed by a modification of the IEP. Thus, if a teacher lacks the skill needed to implement the IEP, or the teacher refuses to implement the IEP, or prevailing expert opinion says the child's participation in extracurricular activities is necessary for educational benefit, the IEP team can require the school to provide appropriately qualified staff, offer compensatory services to make up for deficiencies in IEP implementation caused by the lack of staff training or non-implementation of the IEP, or require the student's participation in extracurricular activities. Thus, the question whether a particular issue is one for the IEP team, or for another decision maker, may need to be reviewed before the IEP team meeting by legal counsel, administration, or an advocate to make sure the IEP team's valuable time is focused on the child's needs and not wasted on some peripheral issue that should be handled elsewhere.

Chapter 2

THE IEP MEETING TO
ADDRESS DISCIPLINE ISSUES

I. BACKGROUND

The central goal in any discipline situation is to determine appropriate consequences that will deter future misconduct and to help the student make better choices. Related goals are to set an example for other students and to keep the learning environment as safe and supportive as possible. The standard "one size fits all" disciplinary consequences in a public school's regular code of conduct may not be the consequences to best achieve these goals for a disabled student whose behavior is the manifestation of a disability. Consequences that substantially interfere with the student's IEP, or bring about a cessation of services, are inappropriate for other reasons and may be unlawful. Consequently, the IEP team, in selecting appropriate consequences for a disabled student who commits a disciplinary infraction, must decide whether the disability caused the behavior or whether the behavior resulted from a deficiency in the child's program, and in either case, what consequence is appropriate for the student. If the disciplinary infraction was not caused by the student's disability, the disciplinary procedures for that infraction that apply to children without disabilities may apply to the disabled child in the same manner, so long as the disciplinary consequences do not involve cessation of services to the child and so long as any disciplinary alternative educational setting where the disabled child is placed can deliver an appropriate IEP for the child. In some cases, the selection of an alternative setting must be made by the IEP team.

IDEA's new discipline provisions narrow the inquiry for determining whether behavior was a manifestation of the child's disability. There is no question now but that the IEP team is the appropriate group of persons to make the manifestation determination. The team specifically must determine: (1) whether the IEP and placement were appropriate in relation to the behavior subject to disciplinary action; (2) whether special education and other services scheduled in the IEP were being provided; (3) whether the child's disability impaired the child's ability to understand the impact and consequences of the behavior; and (4) whether the child's disability impaired the child's ability to control the behavior. In making the manifestation determination, the IEP team must consider "all relevant information" including diagnostic results, relevant information provided by the parents, observations of the child, and the placement and IEP. Incidentally to the manifestation-determination issue, the IEP team also must conduct a functional behavioral assessment to address the behavior that led to the disciplinary referral, or must review the behavior plan if one already was in place, and modify it if necessary.

The impact of the IEP team's decision in discipline situations is often very serious for the child. The IEP team's finding that a student's behavior is not related to the student's disability might result in removal of the student from school, or from the current instructional setting, for a long period of time. Alternatively, the team's decision could result in a significant change of placement and a complete overhaul of the student's IEP. Consequently, decisions regarding discipline are perhaps the most serious decisions an IEP team must make.

The IEP team's legal mandate in making a manifestation determination is to review "all" relevant information. Thus, documentation belonging to the school or in the parent's possession should be brought to the IEP team and carefully considered so that each document, each piece of "evidence," as it were, can be weighed by the team to decide its impact on the team's decision. If the IEP team's decisions must be reviewed later by a judge or hearing officer, the relevant documents will be admitted in evidence for the hearing officer to examine and will speak for themselves. Thus, if the IEP team fails to write down the steps the team followed in considering and weighing each relevant document, the judge or hearing officer will have to make her own decision about the weight and consideration that document was due, and substituting her judgment to fill in for any omission by the IEP team.

II. WHAT DOCUMENTATION SHOULD THE TEAM HAVE AVAILABLE TO CONSIDER, AND WHY?

1. The Most Recent Comprehensive Individual Assessment

This document should contain information for the IEP team to examine concerning the student's behavioral competencies, behavioral deficits, identified disabilities, effects, if any, of disability on behavior, and suggested strategies for addressing any disability-related behaviors. Based on new or updated evidence available to team members, the school or parents may suggest further assessment before the IEP meeting to address behavioral characteristics that may have changed significantly following the last assessment. Further assessment also may be needed where recommendations in the last assessment were implemented, but did not have the expected effect on behavior and and therefore may have been inappropriate. Also, if partial assessments have been completed or submitted to the school after the date of the most recent CIA (e.g. a psychiatric or psychological report), team members will want to consider what effect this new information has on the conclusions and recommendations in the last CIA and, in particular, whether further school-based assessment is needed before the IEP team can make a decision.

2. Parent Records

The IEP team must consider relevant information provided by the parents. Parents often possess documents critical to the IEP team's decision making. Teachers send notes, charts, reports, and logs home with the child containing irreplaceable information pertaining to the child's behavior, but often parents discard this information and teachers fail to maintain copies for their records. Either the school or the parent should be dating and preserving this type of information for purposes of future consideration by the IEP team. Parents often have medical or other assessment reports that they do not think important to share with the school, but that may nonetheless be relevant to the IEP team's manifestation determination. If the child has experienced difficulties in the community, the parent may have possession of or access to critical information from counselors or other officials from the mental health authority, probation authority, or other juvenile offices that can shed light on the linkage question.

3. Teacher Records

Records of general and special education teachers often contain a wealth of "raw" behavioral data that will be of interest to the IEP team. Teacher data includes the observations of the child that are necessary to flesh out a description of behaviors in question. Teacher records may illustrate that the child's IEP is or is not being implemented, or that a particular instructional setting is or is not the appropriate place to implement the child's IEP. Children who are not yet identified for special education eligibility may still be entitled to procedural safeguards, and teacher data is the best source to make judgments about whether the school knew of the child's suspected disability at the time of the incident.

However, teachers rarely recall important details of timing, frequency, duration, and antecedents that describe the contours of classroom behavior incidents. Therefore, teacher notes and other physical records (tokens, sticker sheets, point cards, etc.) are necessary to reconstruct a history of the behavior problem, for interpretation by behavior assessment professionals and other members of the IEP team. Teacher records might include notes home, logs of phone conversations with parents or others regarding specific incidents, check or point sheets, daily behavior records, charts and graphs of behaviors, logs of test grades, student work samples, posters used to describe behavioral expectations or record student progress, and the like. If these records are withheld, lost, or destroyed, the IEP team will not have a clear detailed picture of the behavior in issue, particularly when the teacher's recollection fails and/or the teacher is not available to report to the IEP team.

4. Scheduled Evaluative Data

Another vital source of information comes from records created by teachers, the parents, or the administration in order to comply with evaluation requirements set out in the student's IEP or behavior management plan. It should go without saying that when a previous IEP team called for the creation of certain evaluative data, both parents and school officials should take steps to preserve this data for later consideration by the IEP team.

5. Administrative Records

In many schools, teachers must generate a contact report or referral report when a student is removed from the classroom for office detention, suspension to a disciplinary setting in school, suspension out of school, or time out in another behavior management setting. School administrators likewise generate logs or reports when they must take some administrative action because of student behavior. These records contain essential information about the student's behavioral strengths and deficits, particularly baseline frequencies of disturbing behaviors, information about antecedents, information about consequences and their effects, and information describing behavioral changes over time. An administrative report or police report generated from the incident that triggered the disciplinary referral probably contains the best, most reliable description of that specific behavior the IEP team must analyze in the manifestation determination. This information, along with the student's behavioral and discipline history, is essential to assess characteristic behavior patterns to determine linkage. Teachers and administrators should be taking steps to preserve these educational records according to record retention schedules of state and federal regulations. If parents receive copies of these reports, parents likewise should develop a system for maintaining them. The IEP team and assessment professionals will find these data essential in getting a handle on the nature and severity of behavior problems to help make linkage decisions and conduct mandatory behavioral assessment.

6. School Health Records

Reports by school health officials may contain vital information about health and medical concerns that potentially affect behavior. Where these records are available for inspection by the IEP team, they can help answer questions relevant to the linkage determination including current medications the child may be taking, non-IDEA disabilities of the child (such as ADHD or seizure disorder), and other physical illnesses. While medical conditions of record may or may not be IDEA-qualifying disabilities in and of themselves, they may alter or exacerbate the effects of a disability on behavior. Alternatively, changes in medical conditions may alert the IEP team to the child's need for further assessment for the presence of a new or different IDEA disability. School health personnel who have had involvement with the child should be part of the IEP team and attend or otherwise have input to the IEP meeting to address manifestations of the disability.

7. Related Service Records

Logs, reports, assessments, and other documentation from related service providers can be extremely valuable in making the linkage determination. The records of counseling or psychological services personnel in particular may contain observations, data, and hypotheses relevant to the linkage issue that the IEP team may use, or that may suggest the need for further assessment before making the linkage decision. Related service providers are as much a part of the IEP team as other school professionals and should have input to the decision-making process.

III. WHO SHOULD BE PRESENT AT THE IEP TEAM MEETING TO CONSIDER DISCIPLINE AND WHY?

1. The Parent

The parent's role on the IEP team is to speak for the child, which means insuring that the child's immediate educational and social needs are being addressed appropriately and that short-term and long-term objectives contribute to the child's ability to be a productive citizen. Parents also help insure that procedural safeguards are followed, which should lead to better quality decisions. Parents also provide additional information about a different facet of the child's learning and adjustment that can help other team members understand the causes of the child's behavior. This information includes information about behaviors in the home and community and any other relevant information that has come to the parent's attention of which the school district is unaware.

2. The Child's Special Education Teacher

If the child is eligible for and has been receiving special education, the child's special education teacher has information about the child's current daily functioning: What behaviors are occurring frequently? What sets them off? What modifications and consequences have been attempted or should be attempted? The special education teacher, although usually interacting with the child for a small portion of the school day, is responsible for essential evaluative and monitoring functions, respecting both general and special education, and thus should have an overview of the child's school behavior. The special education teacher sometimes may be asked to serve in the role of "case manager" for the child and thereby may have additional information through contact with the parent and community agencies to communicate to the IEP team. In any case, a special education teacher who works with the child every day, who has specialized training and expertise, who knows about the child's problems, and who has some history of interaction with the child, is an essential member of the IEP team. There is no substitute for this person. If the child's special education teacher is unable to attend the IEP meeting, the teacher must prepare a written report to the IEP team or otherwise send information through a proxy. However, remember that a special education teacher or provider must be present at every IEP meeting. The child's special education teacher should be the person who fulfills this requirement by attending the IEP meeting.

3. The Child's General Education Teacher

For the child whose eligibility is being addressed for the first time in the discipline context, the child who spends part of the school day in general education, or the child who may receive services in general education, the general education teacher is a necessary participant on the IEP team. This individual supplies detailed information about the child's functioning relative to the district's curriculum in appropriate subject-matter areas and relative to other children in the school community. The general education teacher will have accumulated multiple observations of behavioral incidents, along with personal opinions, and from this information can help to flesh out the behavioral analysis of student discipline incidents. The general education teacher can verify and describe the implementation and results of modifications, management strategies, and other supplementary aids and services used in the classroom, to help the team determine whether the behavior resulted from excessive academic frustration due to an inappropriate program. For the child who spends most of the day in special education, and for whom the IEP team suspects this placement may be inappropriate, the general education teacher can help clarify the child's progress, problems, and needs. There is no effective substitute for having the child's general education teacher present at the IEP team meeting. As inclusive practices increase, the typical general education teacher will have more difficulty finding time to attend IEP meetings. Nevertheless, new IDEA requirements will mandate at least one general education teacher's presence at the IEP meeting in most cases. Not every general education teacher of every child will be able to attend the IEP meeting. But it is important that every general education teacher of the child should provide some evaluative information to the IEP team.

4. A School Administrator

A school administrator is required to participate in every IEP meeting. IDEA states that this person must be knowledgeable regarding special education, general education, and the availability of resources within the school. The administrator has several critical tasks on the IEP team that considers the manifestation questions. The administrator usually is the person responsible for investigating the facts behind incidents that trigger discipline referrals. The administrator is the person who reviews and evaluates conflicting evidence, decides what the "facts" are, and makes the initial decision about the appropriate consequence. This means the administrator will know what the evidence tends to show the special education student actually did to warrant disciplinary referral. This administrative data, along with any reports of law enforcement authorities, is usually the best and most reliable description of behavior available to the IEP team that considers linkage.

The administrator also is the person responsible for planning and allocating scarce resources of the school. The administrator must help IEP team members determine the most efficient and effective means to deliver IEP services necessary for the student to receive an appropriate education. The administrator's knowledge and authority provides team members with assurance that the school district stands behind the IEP and will deliver services. Frequently, a disciplinary IEP team meeting will consider a variety of options that may include increasing, decreasing, or modifying the student's general or special education services, and the adminstrator should be involved in the identifying of such options. The administrator also is an instructional leader and in that role is accustomed to working on problem-solving teams. The administrator is the person who resolves disputes and handles other conflict situations where the most fundamental elements of "due process" come into play. These roles often prescribe that the administrator be the leader or chairperson of the IEP team and guide the IEP meeting through the necessary deliberations.

5. The Child's Psychologist

Students with cognitive and/or emotional problems may be at risk to commit disciplinary infractions on a greater frequency than students with other types of disabilities. For such students, the IEP team has the difficult task of considering a possible linkage between the student's behavior and the student's disability-related cognitive and emotional characteristics. Often these students will have been evaluated by a psychologist who works for the school or by a consulting psychologist. Or the student may have received, and may currently be receiving, counseling or therapy from a psychologist. Consequently, the psychologist, by virtue of training in behavioral principles and experience with the student in question, will have a unique role helping the IEP team analyze whether the student's behavior was related to the student's disability or to problems resulting from an inadequate program. The student's psychologist should either participate in IEP team deliberations or else be invited to address the team with a written opinion and recommendations directed to the essential questions for the team's deliberations.

6. Other Assessment Specialists

Disability characteristics take a myriad of forms, and disability - behavior linkage questions can become kaleidoscopic. This is particularly true with neuropsychological disabilities and emotional disabilities, where no single scientific explanation prevails, and several distinct theoretical models coexist offering potentially divergent views about linkage. The IEP team must include an appropriately qualified assessment specialist to interpret assessment and address linkage questions for which assessment is relevant. Did the student's verbal outburst result from Tourette's disorder or a language disability? Further psychiatric and speech evaluations may be necessary. Did the student's violent outburst result from a neurologically based disinhibition syndrome?

Medical and/or neuropsychological assessment may be warranted. With the availability of independent evaluations (or sometimes just because the school's appraisal specialists disagree!), the IEP team may be confronted with two or three "experts" offering different opinions. In any event, the underlying principle is that the IEP team cannot make informed decisions without sufficient input from appraisal specialists with training and experience assessing each and every area of suspected disability.

IV. THE ORDER OF BUSINESS FOR IEP TEAM MEMBERS

1. The Chairperson

Often an administrator is the appropriate person to chair the IEP meeting. In some discipline situations, the administrator may be the focus of so much negative feeling that another team member will need to assume this role. In that case, the school district assessment specialist attending the meeting, such as a school psychologist or other diagnostic specialist, may assume the role of chairperson. Alternatively, if the school district has designated a school employee as a case manager, this person could assume the chair. In any event, the chair should be a person who is acquainted with the child and family, knows about the child's disability and the disciplinary incident, is competent with respect to using IDEA procedural safeguards, and can run a meeting effectively.

2. The Opening

The chair of the IEP meeting should begin by summarizing the purpose of the meeting, indicating in plain terms that decisions will be made concerning appropriate discipline, the linkage between behavior and disability, the linkage between behavior and school placement, and the appropriate future placement. The chair should then tell the participants the proposed order of presentations, including the parent and/or the parent's representatives as well as the school district's representatives. The chair should inquire if the parent received and is satisfied with the notice concerning the time and content of the meeting, understands the order of business and the items for decision, and has any request to alter the agenda, raise additional issues, or present additional information to the team. If the chair fails to so inquire, the parent should raise questions and additional matters at this opening stage of the meeting. Obtaining clarification among all participants at the beginning usually improves efficiency, as well as the likelihood that no important matters are overlooked for discussion and documentation by the school district and the parent.

3. Presenting Assessment Information and Identifying Present Competencies

The first item of business in the discipline IEP meeting is to discuss current assessment. Current assessment includes the most recent comprehensive individual assessment; any formal assessment update completed since the most recent CIA; teacher assessment, formal and informal, of present academic competencies; and any assessment data presented by the parent including parent observations and behavioral data, as well as any independent or outside evaluation submitted by the parent. Any IEP team member who has assessment data should present a brief overview of that data, followed by a summary of impressions, conclusions, and recommendations. Conclusions will include an opinion regarding whether the behavior in question is related to the student's disability, according to the person responsible for the assessment.

4. Examining the Current Eligibility

Based on assessment conclusions and recommendations the IEP team needs to identify the current IDEA disability or disabilities. In the case of mental, emotional, and/or behavior disorders, it is not appropriate for the team to attempt a psychological or medical "diagnosis" of the child. Rather, the team should rely on the conclusions of appropriately trained and certified assessment professionals. Typically one or more of four possibilities will exist at this stage. (1) The available assessments may be both acceptable to all team members and definitive with respect to a diagnosis. Here, the team can use recommendations of the assessment professional and other sources to identify the kinds of behaviors likely to "manifest" the diagnosis, as well as to generate appropriate objectives and strategies for that diagnosis. (2) The school may have its own definitive assessment, but that assessment's conclusions and recommendations may provoke the parent to disagree with the school's assessment and request a "second opinion." In that case, the team should identify the specific areas of disagreement, recess the team meeting, obtain an appropriate independent assessment, and then consider both assessments in subsequent deliberations. (3) The available assessments may be ambiguous or silent with respect to the existence or status of a new condition or disability that team members have reason to suspect is present. Here, the IEP team must recess to obtain additional assessment, addressing the proper referral question, and then consider that additional assessment in future deliberations. (4) The team may have two or more current assessment reports that reach different conclusions. For example, this would be true when the results of the school's assessment conflict with assessment obtained by the parent or from an independent evaluator. In this scenario, the team must consider several factors including the prevalence, within education settings, of behaviors and other characteristics relied upon by the respective assessment professionals, the extensiveness of the observations and other data gathered by the different professionals, and the experience and qualifications of the different professionals, and then make a decision about which assessment is more reliable. It is always important to consider whether the methods and procedures used in a particular assessment comply with federal guidelines and regulations as well as professional standards. The team then should use the more reliable assessment for further deliberations, eligibility determination, and manifestation determination.

5. Examining the Behavior-Disability Linkage

The team is responsible to determine if the student's behavior for which disciplinary action has been proposed is related to the student's disability. Court decisions have indicated that this relationship, or linkage, must be direct and causal. Indirect, attenuated links between behavior and disability are not sufficient to satisfy this standard. IDEA now explains that student behavior may be linked to the student's disability if the disability impaired the child's ability to understand the "impact and consequences" of the behavior or whether the disability impaired the child's ability to control the behavior. The development of state and federal regulations, as well as future court decisions, will no doubt help to explain how schools should interpret the new IDEA standard.

As with eligibility decisions, the IEP team making a manifestation determination is in no position to evaluate linkage without the input of someone with expertise in the student's disability who can submit an opinion to the team about this issue. If the student has a psychological disability, the psychologist needs to state an opinion for the team. If the student has a neurological disability, a neurologist or neuropsychologist should do this job. The IEP team's judgment is always limited by the quality of "evidence" put before the team. Bad information yields bad decisions. The team's options with respect to assessment are the same regardless of the domain of disputed assessment, depending on whether the team has definitive assessment, disputed assessment, ambiguous assessment, or conflicting assessments.

6. Examining the IEP and Its Implementation

The next step will be to consider the appropriateness of the current IEP, in light of the most recent agreed-upon formal and informal assessment and the assessment recommendations.

Procedural Compliance

The team must address several threshold procedural questions. Were the current IEP and the recent past IEPs developed in conformity with IDEA's procedural safeguards, including notice to the parent, parent consent for initial assessment, initial placement, and any other activity for which parent consent is required by law, and participation by the parent or parent surrogate? If these procedural requirements were not met, there exists a strong possibility that the IEP may be inappropriate, and the team must immediately consider strategies for remedying identified procedural deficiencies. If these requirements were met, then the team must consider two other procedural issues. First, is the assessment current with respect to compliance with regulatory requirements and with respect to the evaluation of all suspected disabilities? Second, were scheduled IEP services actually delivered? If assessment is not current, the team needs to schedule any needed assessment that is appropriate before attempting to make a linkage decision. If IEP services were not being delivered, there once again exists the strong presumption that procedural rights were breached and the team must immediately consider what steps are necessary to repair the breach.

Current assessment support

Once procedural questions are resolved, the IEP team must evaluate whether current assessment recommendations support the IEP with respect to specific academic and behavioral objectives, type and amount of related services, assistive technology, and supplementary aids and services needed for appropriate mainstreaming. The team should ask, do goals, objectives, and services make sense? do they fit the characteristics of the current identified IDEA handicapping condition? do they also fit the characteristics of the current psychological, psychiatric, or neurological diagnosis, if any? If the IEP team can say with confidence that these criteria were met, then the IEP is probably an appropriate one with respect to goals, objectives, and services.

Student Progress

But is the student making progress under that IEP? Teacher input concerning the student's present competencies and progress since the time of the last IEP review should largely answer this question. Here, teacher records and other data should be available to support the teacher's subjective opinion and provide tangible proof of what the student is achieving in class and how that establishes progress.

Least Restrictive Environment

The next question for the team is whether the IEP is being implemented in the least restrictive environment (LRE) that is possible and appropriate in light of the extent of required services, as well as the goals and objectives that can be or must be implemented in mainstream settings. The process for the IEP team's consideration of LRE is covered in a separate section of this booklet. The reader is directed to that section for guidance in addressing the appropriateness mainstreaming provided in the IEP.

7. Examining the Behavior-IEP Linkage

At this juncture, the team will have reached conclusions about whether the current IEP and the extent of mainstreaming are or are not appropriate for the student. If the team feels that the IEP is appropriate, the team has no need to examine a possible link between the behavior in question and an inappropriate placement or IEP. However, if the team finds or suspects shortcomings in the IEP, the question then becomes whether the deficiencies in the IEP caused the behavior that triggered the proposed discipline. If there are procedural deficiencies such as a failure to provide required notice to the parent, the proper course of action will be to deliver proper notice and then convene the IEP team after proper notice to consider disputed issues. If, however, the IEP deficiencies have substantive implications, i.e. failure to have current assessment, failure to deliver scheduled IEP services failure to address recommendations in the current assessment, or failure to deliberate carefully the provision or omission of an IEP service or placement, then the team should examine whether the deficiency was a cause of the behavior. The psychologist or other assessment professional on the team should be prepared to state an opinion about how a student with this type of disability might react to stresses caused by an inappropriate placement or inappropriate IEP services, and how the student in question would be expected to react. If the expected reaction matches the student's behavior in question, then the team may conclude that there exists a direct relationship between the student's behavior and the inappropriateness of the IEP or placement. If different experts on the team state differing opinions on his point, the team must take steps to decide which professional opinion is more reliable, then base a linkage determination on that opinion.

V. KEY DELIBERATIONS TO DOCUMENT

Any point worth serious discussion by the IEP team merits at least some passing mention in the written minutes of the team's deliberations. Any point that might be the subject of appeal to an impartial hearing officer certainly should be documented carefully. If the team's decisions are later disputed or appealed, the written record can help to establish what went on in the meeting, even if the key players have moved on to other positions, become unavailable for some other reason, or cannot independently remember what took place in the deliberations. Tape recording the team's deliberations may be a good idea in principle, but in reality is rarely an adequate substitute for written minutes of deliberations. Recordings are often of poor quality, get lost or destroyed, or cannot be heard and understood because the team is engaging in lively debate and several people are talking at once. The written minutes of the team's deliberations thus should document all key points. Of particular importance, the team will want to ensure an unambiguous record of several essential points. (1) Do members agree, or disagree, with respect to current assessment findings and recommendations? If not, then which specific findings and recommendations are agreed upon and which are not agreed upon? (2) Is further assessment necessary? If so, what kind of assessment, how will it be done, and what are the time lines for finishing it? And when will the team next convene to consider the results? (3) If members have rejected certain recommendations of the current assessment as inappropriate but are not recommending further assessment, what are the specific reasons for rejecting certain recommendations and accepting others? (4) As to the key linkage questions, what is the opinion of each team member on the ultimate questions? (5) Finally, what is the consensus of the team on each linkage question and the appropriate specific steps that must be taken?

VI. INVOKING STOP-GAP MEASURES

As with any other type of IEP team dispute, the team may recess the discipline IEP meeting, as touched upon in the preceding discussion of IDEA procedural options, at any point the team feels further assessment is needed, or additional documentation or references need to be reviewed, or outside persons need to be consulted or invited to be part of the team, or merely because tensions need time to wind down. Often a recess, possibly coupled with informal alternative dispute resolution, allows the team members who are in disagreement to find alternatives that will resolve the impasse and produce an acceptable solution, as well as an appropriate IEP for the student.

Chapter 3

THE IEP MEETING TO ADDRESS PLACEMENT IN THE LEAST RESTRICTIVE EDUCATIONAL SETTING

I. BACKGROUND

School representatives facing administrative problems, and parents seeking either normalized opportunities for their children or special opportunities in special classrooms, may approach the IEP meeting with a pre-existing preference for a particular instructional setting. They deliberate around that setting, selecting or discarding goals and services, mainly to justify the setting. Consequently, the team's placement discussions usually meander far from the process contemplated in special education law. Then, as weeks pass and the student's progress grinds to a halt, the IEP team has to reconvene, maybe several times, trying to "fine tune" a placement that really needs an overhaul. Occasionally due process has to be invoked to repair the IEP, and that can cost more than a visit from your plumber.

Congress has supplied the authoritative blueprint for LRE decision making. Congress explained that "to the maximum extent appropriate, children with disabilities...are educated with children who are non-disabled." Furthermore, special classes, special schools, or other types of removal of children with disabilities from the regular education classroom may occur only "when the nature and severity of the disability is such that education in regular classes, with the use of supplementary aids and services cannot be achieved satisfactorily." Preservation of this ideal in the reauthorized IDEA testifies to the validity of its premise. Congressional blueprints, as they are processed through various committees, often lose practical information they once may have contained. Even so, the LRE clause is one of IDEA's few substantive provisions and thus is a key expression of legislative purpose.

28

Courts charged with repairing LRE malfunctions have interpreted the LRE clause by designing more utilitarian models for how to make LRE decisions. Two of these models have gained wide acceptance around the nation. You should study the law that applies in your jurisdiction to make sure you understand the operating procedures for your particular model. But the models are built upon fundamental concepts you should study before you try to tinker with placement. It will be important to quickly review these concepts before discussing how to make LRE decisions.

Goals and Services Go Before Placement

The IEP team must write appropriate goals and services that deliver FAPE for the child, before tackling the LRE decision of where to implement the program. This entails: (1) determining appropriate regluar curriculum objectives and identifying aids and services that are necessary for the child to attain those objectives; (2) selecting appropriate and comprehensive special education academic, behavioral, and other developmental objectives that will confer meaningful benefit; and (3) identifying the services necessary to achieve each of those special education objectives during the time period covered by the IEP.

Once this is done, the IEP team has before it (1) a description of the aids and services necessary to educate the child in the regular curriculum, to the extent appropriate; (2) a list of academic IEP objectives that may require special education; (2) a description of the type and amount of services necessary to achieve special education objectives; (3) a description of related services necessary for the child to benefit from special education; and (5) a list of non-academic (e.g. behavioral, social, developmental) objectives along with the services needed to achieve them. Only with a list of objectives and necessary services in hand is the team prepared to consider whether any need exists for removing the child from the regular education setting.

The IEP team must approach this process of goal-setting and service-identification from a foundation of current assessment. This means assessment of academic functioning by the classroom teacher, and assessment of functioning in any other area where the team believes the child needs objectives and services, by an individual with expertise in that area. Readers are urged to review the chapter pertaining to selection of appropriate goals and objectives for further information.

The Mainstream Is Presumed Appropriate

Special education law presumes that the regular education class-room is the appropriate setting to educate every child. The practical effect of this presumption is, if the IEP team contemplates removing a child from that setting, for any instruction or other service, there must be good cause shown that such removal is necessary to provide the child with an appropriate education.

If the child is currently being educated in the mainstream for one or more academic subjects and the IEP team is considering removing the child from the mainstream for some period of time, how might the team establish that this is necessary? What concerns might the team have? The team has already done the most prudent groundwork by actually attempting placement in regular education, with the support of a full range of supplementary aids and services. If the team is concerned that the child is not being successful, the team should first examine carefully the nature and extent of supplementary aids and services to see if a change in services, or a reasonable increase in services, might make the mainstream successful.

In any event, the evaluative information flowing from a mainstream placement helps to tell the IEP team whether and to what extent main-stream placement can be successful in the future and what services might be needed to make it so. Alternatively, this information can demon-strate why it is not feasible for the school to deliver appropriate educa-tion to the child in that setting.

But what if the child's current placement is in special education? And the child is being successful there? Is it still necessary to consider mainstream placement? Regardless of the child's last successful place-ment, every LRE deliberation should begin with a discussion of the pros and cons of regular education placement as the first point of depar-ture. The team should be convinced by that discussion and should clearly explain in the deliberations why it is not feasible to make a main-stream placement succeed for the child, even with a substantial commit-ment of appropriate aids and services. Starting LRE deliberations by discussing placement in the regular education setting helps keep the team grounded with respect to the purpose and significance of LRE.

Feasibility and Other Murky Questions

The IEP team's overriding concern is to provide the child with appropriate education, that is, with objectives and services that meet the child's individual needs. The essence of the LRE decision is, "Can those objectives and services be realized 'satisfactorily' in the regular education setting, given the nature and severity of the disability?" Another way of stating this is to ask whether it is "feasible" for the school to deliver an appropriate program in the mainstream. Courts have approached this issue of "satisfactory" implementation in limited ways, but nevertheless have given IEP teams what guidance presently exists for addressing the issue.

One fairly well-settled principle is that it is not "feasible" to implement a child's program in the mainstream setting, if doing so would disrupt the education of all students in that setting. But what kind of "disruption" is the law talking about here? If the child has very severe behavior problems that directly interfere with instruction, those problems might create disruption serious enough to require placement outside the mainstream. Children who frequently scream, throw objects, take off their clothes, destroy classroom property, assault staff or students, or try to stop the teacher or other students from working, likely requires specialized care outside the mainstream if normal behavior management strategies cannot quickly bring such behaviors under control.

Disruption, in the legal sense of that term, also might occur if the program that the child needs in order to benefit from school is very different from the instructional needs of other children in the classroom. The differences may be so great that the child requires the full attention of the classroom teacher in order to implement her program correctly. In such cases, it also may be true that the child's program requires staff with expertise and training not possessed by regular education (or in some cases even resource special education) or specially certified staff. The child's needs for additional one on one instruction, as well as special materials, methods and curriculum, will affect placement deliberations.

Or it may not be "feasible" to implement a special program in the regular classroom setting in instances where the program is the placement. That is, the child literally may require a specially designed environment that may not be compatible with the regular classroom. For example, successful interventions for certain severely mentally handicapped students require a high level of staff expertise and elaborate environmental controls that may not be compatible with a regular classroom. Furthermore, such programs often operate "level" systems where the child earns access to the regular classroom as reality orientation and behavior problems improve. Likewise, children with certain types of cognitive disabilities may need exposure to environments so highly stimulating that the environment is not compatible with teaching any academic curriculum.

Thus, for a small number of children, such as those with severe behavior problems, profound cognitive disabilities, and/or elaborate medical needs, the team must study the potential impact of the child's needs on both the child and the other students in the regular classroom. If instruction and/or the social milieu of the classroom will be disrupted significantly, the child in question is not likely to obtain academic and non-academic benefits there. Other children will lose their educational opportunity as well. In such a case, mainstream placement would probably be inappropriate. But IEP teams must keep in mind that, in the early grades, many regular classroom curriculum objectives, including objectives aimed at socializing the child to the school setting, will be appropriate for children with severe disabilities, even children who show little capacity to respond to the environment or acquire basic behavioral skills.

Comparing the Benefits of Alternative Settings

The hardest part of the IEP team's charge boils down to balancing the anticipated benefits and detriments to the child of each alternative setting where it would be feasible to deliver necessary services, for each curriculum area and related domain where the child needs instruction. If the team anticipates to propose some removal from the regular education setting, there must be a clear statement of reasons why a genuine commitment of aids and services in that setting will still not enable the child to receive appropriate education there. What are some "typical" considerations of this balancing process?

If a child's presence in the regular education setting is not disruptive, and the child functions to some extent on the same level as other children in the classroom, then it seems a relatively easy step to place the child in that classroom. The child will be performing some subset of general curriculum objectives alongside non-disabled peers and benefitting from exposure to social and behavioral expectations of that setting. The child will need only enough support (in the regular education classroom or elsewhere) to cover general curriculum objectives the child has not mastered, learn compensatory strategies to cope with skills the child is not expected to master, or obtain support in related non-academic domains.

If the child's presence in the regular education setting is not disruptive but the child functions on a much different level than others in the classroom, such that few or none of the general curriculum objectives of that classroom are appropriate, the LRE decision is more complex. The IEP team must somehow try to balance conflicting concerns in the child's education. For example, is it more important for this child at this time to have opportunities to acquire social and behavioral skills from interacting with non-disabled peers, or is it more important now to have intensive one-on-one instruction from a teacher to learn skills in academic and non-academic deficiency areas? The child's age, the nature and severity of the disability, and the anticipated long-term transition goals identified by the IEP team will factor in the decision. IEP teams will likely have to shift the balance as the child ages, her abilities change or stabilize, and the IEP team commences formal transition planning. The nature, availability, and appropriateness of extended services, such as extended school year, creates options that may affect the choice of learning experiences and settings during the regular school year .

In comparing the array of services and modifications that may benefit the child in one setting versus another, the IEP team often is forced to prioritize appropriate goals and objectives. Is developing social skills and self-esteem more important today than learning algebra or how to balance a checkbook? The law does not require IEP teams to "maximize" benefit here but rather to try and view the child's needs from different perspectives her current developmental level, her motivation, the nature of her disability, the curriculum expectations of her age cohort, and the best estimate of which long-term goals she should strive for to achieve independence in tomorrow's world. The IEP team's integration of these perspectives guides the selection of objectives and instructional setting to advance the child toward attaining necessary skills.

Assessment in critical areas, properly done and with an eye to transition planning, can aid this complex process. Yet, deciding the LRE for these children, who are not disruptive but who also do not "fit" the general classroom, will always be a difficult process. Your IEP teams cannot ignore the law in your jurisdiction for guiding the LRE decision and indeed should be proficient in applying the key points. But realize also that the law cannot possibly make a rule adequate for every child or every classroom, and the judgment of professional educators, particularly when supported by independent experts, may be the most reliable guidance.

Exhaust All Avenues of Mainstreaming

After the team has settled on objectives, prioritized them, identified all necessary services, and deliberated to agreement on the least restrictive setting for delivering those services, the team's last job is to ask whether all possible avenues for mainstreaming have been exhausted. This includes capitalizing on non-instructional time (lunch breaks, bathroom breaks), elective or "non-academic" courses, and other opportunities during the school day for appropriate mainstreaming during "free" time, mentoring, or as a reward for effort.

What About Cost?

If schools had unlimited resources, it might be possible to "satisfactorily" implement special education in the mainstream for a great many more children with disabilities. How, then, is the IEP team to address the issue of cost? At what point does escalating cost of supplementary aids and services render mainstream placement not feasible or satisfactory for a child who otherwise might obtain benefit? If the child will benefit from mainstream placement all day, or all morning, or for language arts, it is necessary for the school to hire additional staff to assist the regular classroom teacher, or purchase an expensive communication device or interpreter, or obtain costly training for the teacher? Must the team choose the objectives and services of the mainstream setting over some other set of objectives and services that can be achieved at less cost (or with greater economic efficiency) in a segregated setting or a mainstream setting at a campus other than the campus the child would attend if non-disabled?

Congress did not tell local school districts or state education agencies what proportion of their budget to allocate for students with disabilities, as opposed to other groups of nondisabled students such as limited English proficiency students, minority students, gifted students, disadvantaged students, or students with no special status at all. Congress has, however, indirectly told schools to look at cost very carefully in making special education decisions. Congress granted students with disabilities potent procedural rights, including the right to reimbursement of the student's attorney's fees if the student wins a hearing. Courts have further ordered schools to pay for private education in cases where the school refuses or is unable to provide appropriate placement. These rights carry a high price tag that schools must consider when assessing the cost of different placement options.

The courts, lacking specific guidance from lawmakers, have backed away from writing decisions that require schools to "maximize" benefit for children with disabilities or mandate a certain formula for deciding what schools have to spend on disabled students. It is left to local districts and state agencies to decide the essentially political questions of how to divide limited taxpayer dollars. Under present federal funding, it is these state and local dollars that fund the "nuts and bolts" of special education. That much said, courts have tended to shy away from requiring schools to hire one teacher or nurse to service only one disabled child or to purchase unusually expensive medical equipment. But beyond this minimal guidance, schools are left on their own to decide what services are "feasible" for delivering appropriate education in the LRE.

Documentation belonging to the school or in the parent's possession should be presented to the IEP team so that each document, each piece of "evidence" as it were, can be considered and weighed by the team to decide its impact on the team's decision. The IEP team is legally responsible to consider and to use in a rational way all relevant information needed to arrive at an appropriate placement decision. If the IEP team's decisions must be reviewed later by a judge or hearing officer, all relevant documents will be admitted in evidence for the hearing officer to examine, and it will speak for themselves. Thus, if the IEP team fails to write down the steps the team followed in considering and weighing each relevant document, the judge or hearing officer will not hesitate to make her own decision about the weight and consideration that document was due, substituting her judgment to fill in for any omission by the IEP team.

II. WHAT DOCUMENTATION SHOULD THE TEAM HAVE AVAILABLE TO CONSIDER, AND WHY?

1. The Most Recent Comprehensive Individual Assessment

The CIA and supporting assessments should guide the team in selecting appropriate objectives, estimating the progress feasible during the time period covered by the IEP, and identifying what services are necessary to achieve that progress. Physical assessment identifies sensory, motor, and physical characteristics that may affect school progress and may require specific services. Language assessment identifies competencies, abilities, and deficits, affecting school performance in the broadest way, that may require specific objectives and services. Sociological background further highlights social and adaptive deficits or differences that may require educational or non academic related objectives and training. Intellectual assessment helps the team estimate what progress might be expected in various domains of cognitive functioning. Academic assessment, of the normative variety, shows the committee whether skill deficits alone are so severe as to require learning disability services. The "product" of the CIA, namely, the type of eligibility, the nature of the underlying disability, and the needed services and estimate of expected progress, outline the foundation on which the IEP team must build a program of services and then decide where to implement it.

2. Parent Records

Documents in the parent's possession are necessary and important to consider in deciding the child's LRE. The parents may, for example, have data essential to consider the child's behavioral and physical health needs, such as reports of counselors, law enforcement authorities, mental health providers, or medical providers. The diligent parent who has retained disciplinary referral information over a long period of time may possess the only chronicle of the child's more serious in school behavior problems for programming and evaluation purposes. That parent also may have retained teacher notes and other information sent home with the child containing valuable history. The parent who has worked at home attempting to address the child's learning difficulties may have both work samples and irreplaceable insights about what the child can do and what techniques and reinforcers are helpful.

3. Teacher Records

Teacher grade information, behavior logs, notes, work sheets, work samples, tests, and other evaluative records, from both regular and special education, are necessary to consider in order to get a picture of the child's strengths, deficits, and needs related to the disability. The records of a diligent teacher also should contain information about methods and strategies that the teacher has used, along with the success or failure of those methods in teaching the child. Teacher records often contain valuable behavioral data for assessment purposes and notes or other information about social and environmental experiences, in or out of school, that may be affecting the child's classroom adjustment and performance.

4. Scheduled Evaluative Data

Standardized test data, teachers' grade books, the child's scores on individual quizzes and graded assignments, and behavioral data will all be important for the team to examine in deliberating about a placement change. Daily grades and work sheets, for example, show the team concretely where the child functions compared to daily expectations for the class as a whole and what additional help or modifications the child needs. This is essential information in deciding the type and amount of services to provide and how much removal from the mainstream, if any, is necessary to deliver the services. All evaluative information regularly maintained by the teacher and/or collected by the parent are relevant and potentially can shed light on the placement issue. Therefore, the team should account for this information.

5. Administrative Records

Records collected by the campus disciplinarian, counselor, and nurse can be helpful in assessing the success of the child's placement. For example, in one fairly common scenario, the child appears struggling to maintain and does maintain acceptable scholastic performance, but office referrals or trips to the school nurse suggest the stress is taking a toll on the child's emotional adjustment. The committee obviously will want to consider this information in deciding the current placement's appropriateness. Or another example. The teacher recommends that the "difficult" child be removed from her classroom to the resource room because of behavior problems. However, no behaviors have occurred serious enough to warrant the teacher referring the child to the campus counselor or discipline official, and indeed, the teacher has no daily record of any kind to show the team that any serious problems exist. Compare that situation with the situation of the teacher who has made emergency requests for office assistance three out of four afternoons per week for the last six weeks because of carefully-documented incidents in which the child has panic attacks, yells at imaginary people, and strikes himself and others with his fists. This documentation could trigger several interventions by the IEP team, including consideration of a placement change. Thus, the careful creation, retention, and evaluation of administrative records may become critically important.

6. School Health Records

These records should be updated and examined periodically along with other evaluative data to determine if the child has a condition that interferes with scholastic performance. This information, perhaps supplemented with clarification from the parent, should enable the IEP team to determine what supplementary aids and services may be necessary, as well as the appropriate setting to deliver any appropriate services.

7. Related Service Records

The IEP team needs to consider evaluative data and progress records of related service providers, if any, before considering a change of placement for the child. A problem with the nature or amount of related service may be contributing to adjustment or learning problems in the regular classroom, but the members of the IEP team are not aware of the related service issues because of communication lapse among the professionals. A change in the type or amount of related service should be considered, being one additional type of aid or service to help the child succeed in the mainstream. If the related service provider is not available to help other team members interpret related service records, then someone on the team, for example, an assessment professional, can talk with the related service provider to obtain clarification and specific recommendations for other members of the team.

III. WHO SHOULD BE PRESENT AT THE IEP TEAM MEETING TO CONSIDER LRE AND WHY?

1. The Parent

The LRE decision is one of the most complex decisions IEP teams have to make, because it requires knowledge of curriculum, disability characteristics, learning characteristics, necessary professional services, and the appropriate methods for engineering successful learning environments. Many parents who are not educators may not have the time or resources to fully inform themselves on these issues. Many others develop considerable expertise relative to the child's disability and educational issues, not to mention special education law! Yet, even though LRE issues tend to be more expert-driven than many parents care to deal with, the real test of any piece of data or recommendation put before the committee is not what the committee thinks of the proponent, but whether the data or recommendations are sound, based on adequate scientific or clinical research, and relevant to the child's needs. Even parents who are less interested in LRE issues still have a vital role to play, in at least two respects. The parent imposes an important check on the accuracy of data on which the IEP team relies. That is, the parent can demand a "second opinion" with respect to any questionable assessment or expert opinion the school offers to support a proposed placement, simply by requesting an independent evaluation. The parent also speaks as the advocate for the child, and in that vital role, the mere attentive presence of an involved parent acts as an "insurance policy" tending to encourage the district's best efforts to find the least restrictive placement. Of course, as an advocate and legal representative, the parent has a duty to express to the committee the placement preference that the parent reasonably believes to be in the child's best interest.

The parent participates in the IEP meeting as the advocate and representative of the best interests of the child and tells the team about goals and expectations for the child's future toward which educators should be working. The parent exercises procedural rights that insure the IEP team bases its decision on current, valid information. Parents (as well as educators) often bring strong preferences to the IEP team regarding placement, either in the mainstream or in a special setting.

Sometimes these preferences are based on personal feelings, the experiences of the child's siblings or other children, or professional recommendations of outside experts with varying backgrounds. Keeping in mind the law's presumption in favor of the mainstream, the other members of the IEP team must hear the parent out and consider any expert advice the parent brings. Ultimately, the team has to decide the weight, meaning the degree of import and relevance, to be accorded parent preference and expert opinion in balancing the various factors that can spell success or failure for the child in a particular setting. As with all IEP decisions, the team studies the qualifications of the person making the recommendation, considers whether the recommendation is consistent with other information before the committee, and asks if the recommendation, even though not exactly supported by expert opinion, still makes sense in light of all the information available to the team.

2. The Child's Special Education Teacher

If the child is receiving special education services and the IEP team needs to discuss whether to increase or decrease services, the special education teacher can offer direct information about the child's current functioning from the perspective of special education. Specifically, this teacher will be attuned to the appropriate special methodologies for addressing the disability, the types of aids and services that may be available to support mainstream placement, and the pros and cons of removing the child from the mainstream for special education services. The teacher also may be aware of non-educational services available to the child and family. Because of this knowledge and background, the special education teacher also will have important information to give the IEP team considering options for serving a child who is fully mainstreamed with appropriate aids and services as well as special education.

3. The Child's Regular Education Teacher

Evaluative information supplied by a regular classroom teacher who has worked with the child is singularly important information in the LRE decision. That is why IDEA now requires the attendance of a regular education teacher at the IEP meeting of every special education student who receives or may receive mainstream instruction. If the teacher knows the child, the teacher will be familiar with the child's functioning relative to the regular education curriculum and the classroom setting. The teacher is the only professional with direct knowledge of what skills the child has, or is learning, compared to others in the classroom; what special techniques or materials enable the child to learn; and what kinds of experiences motivate the child to accept challenges. This is not information that can be obtained by standardized testing or from outside experts, who are limited to discrete observations and educated inferences. Even if the child is not currently in the mainstream setting, the team can obtain vital information from a regular education teacher who either worked with the child in the past or who simply knows the regular education learning environment. In any event, if the team anticipates moving the child into a mainstream setting, the team must have the input of the regular teacher who may be working with the child. That teacher is in the best position to help the IEP team choose the type and amount of special education support and select appropriate modifications to curriculum and instruction. It should be clear by now why the IEP team must obtain input from the regular education teacher.

The regular education teacher or teachers who know the child and the proposed mainstream setting also will be familiar with the needs of other children with disabilities and non-disabled children in that setting and how the education of those children might be affected by changing the amount of regular education for the child in question. The teacher will be able to explain to the committee the classroom setting as well as explaining classroom methodologies and the supplementary aids and services available in the classroom. These are crucial facts for making the LRE decision.

4. A School Administrator

The school administrator often is responsible, along with the special education teacher or appraisal specialist, for conducting the IEP team meeting to see that all procedural steps are addressed and every member has a chance to speak on the issues. The administrator also serves as the official representative of the school district providing assurance that the district will allocate resources to implement the IEP. The administrator may or may not have additional expertise to aid the committee in addressing difficult professional issues and making an appropriate placement. As with other team members, the administrator has an important role to play, but substantive information from any team member has to be weighed in light of that member's professional training and background, as well as the experience they bring to bear as educators and their knowledge of the child. This principle applies to school administrators as well as other team participants.

5. The Psychologist or Behavior Specialist

If the child is proposed for a placement change and problem behaviors are part of the reason, including behaviors related to the child's motivation and classroom participation, the IEP team should include the school district's psychologist or behavior specialist. Any proposed placement change triggered by disciplinary infractions requires that the school conduct, or update, a functional assessment of the behavior in question. The psychologist or other professional should review all pertinent documentation, conduct one or more structured classroom observation and be prepared to advise the team regarding what strategies if any would be appropriate to assist the child in a mainstream placement and what comparative benefits exist in the various alternative settings where the child might be educated appropriately. The psychologist also will have reviewed the current comprehensive assessment, considered the implications of that assessment for the child's expected learning characteristics, and determined whether the child may need a further formal assessment update in one or more domains in order for the IEP team to have accurate current information.

6. Other Assessment Specialists

Educational appraisal specialists may become involved in reviewing current testing and, if necessary, working with the teacher to bring curriculum-referenced assessment up to date in situations where the child's academic performance is one of the considerations for the IEP team in comparing alternative placements. This is particularly true where the teacher or parent identifies the need for another professional opinion regarding the child's academic potential. Professionals with expertise in assessing other domains of functioning, such as related service professionals, may need to become involved to the extent their area of expertise is implicated among the reasons justifying a proposal to change the child's placement. A person must be present at the IEP team meeting who can interpret assessment results that are relevant to the team's deliberations.

7. Related Service Professionals

As indicated earlier, related services may in some cases be part of the supplementary aids and services the school must provide to support a regular education placement. Assessing the likelihood that providing a related service will succeed in giving the needed support can, in many cases, only be done by the related service professional after consultation with the teacher regarding the child's specific needs. In other situations, the LRE issue will directly concern the delivery of the related service itself - whether it can and should be delivered in the regular classroom or in a different setting. Again, the team must consider the feasibility of delivering the service in the regular classroom, including any disruptive effect on the learning environment, and must compare the benefits to the child of delivering the service in an alternative setting versus the regular classroom. The expert opinion of the related service provider herself, as well as other professionals, will provide the foundation for the team's decision.

IV. THE ORDER OF BUSINESS FOR IEP TEAM MEMBERS

1. The Chairperson

The chair of the IEP meeting to discuss placement should be someone very familiar with the law pertaining to LRE, including the general principles set out in this book as well as any additional issues and factors to consider under the case law in your jurisdiction. The role of the chair in a placement IEP team meeting, in addition to being a facilitator of the meeting, will be to make sure that all the necessary agenda items are discussed and the deliberations documented. Thus, the chair should be able to perform this function with confidence, or else make sure someone is present at the meeting who can. If the regular education administrator is the chair, this person may or may not have sufficient professional training and background to make sure all bases are covered. A special education administrator, supervisor, or assessment professional, or in some cases the child's case manager, should be available and either chair the meeting or take control of the meeting to guide placement deliberations, particularly when it is expected that issues will be complex or contested.

2. The Opening

After the team members are introduced, the chair or designee should carefully explain any action proposed by the school or by the parent, so that everyone in attendance understands what is being proposed. If the meeting is called only to begin exploration of alternative settings because of a problem such as the child's failure to progress, or an escalation of behavior problems, and members of the team have no specific placement proposal in mind at the outset of the meeting, this also should be explained. However, at some point in the opening comments, the chair or another person needs to emphasize that a change of placement to one or more specific alternative settings might be discussed in the meeting along with other options.

3. Presenting Assessment Information and Identifying Present Competencies

The team leader must elicit comments from participants regarding current formal and informal assessment and the present academic and behavioral competencies of the child. The discussion of present competencies should lead a specific description of the child's deficits, problem areas, and strengths, prompting a recommendation for a change of services including any change to a more restrictive or less restrictive setting.

4. Examining the Current Eligibility

For an IEP to be coherent and consistent with professional "best practices," it must provide services that professionals tend to agree are appropriate for the child's condition and eligibility classification. At the same time, many special education services and modifications can benefit a wide variety of mild to moderately disabled children, regardless of eligibility classification. Thus, eligibility is not usually a pressing issue for placement decisions. However, local policies may make eligibility an issue if the school district has created "categorical" programs that ostensibly are open only to children with a certain eligibility, such as autism or "multiply disabled." This is not the place to debate the wisdom of such an approach, except to note that specialized programs may be useful, particularly for children with certain severe disabilities, to concentrate the expertise of highly specialized staff and other resources or else carry out programs that cannot be implemented successfully in the regular education setting because the program requires a special setting. If the team feels strongly that the child requires the services of a particular program but lacks the "required" eligibility, perhaps the team should recess to obtain additional assessment. The rationale for having a separate educational program of this nature ordinarily is related to the child's needs for certain specialized services services that cannot be delivered effectively in the regular classroom rather than to an eligibility classification.

5. Determining Necessary Special Education Services

The child's assessment data, eligibility, and present academic and behavioral competencies, including problem areas, should lead to recommendations concerning what services are necessary for the child to obtain meaningful benefit on regular curriculum or on IEP objectives. If the members of the team agree on the necessary types and amounts of services, being careful to distinguish what is necessary from what is helpful but not necessary, the discussion can shift smoothly to examine alternative settings where those services can be implemented successfully.

6. Identifying and Comparing Settings Where Services Can Be Implemented

Once the team has resolved any disagreements about appropriate services, the team is ready to elicit specific recommendations of each team member regarding where those services should be implemented. Remember, the regular classroom setting is presumed to be appropriate, and will be found appropriate, unless the team explains why the IEP cannot be satisfactorily implemented there with the use of supplementary aids and services. If the assessments, present competencies, and deliberations regarding educational need have been done carefully, then the groundwork has been laid for the team to make a straightforward decision. Sometimes, however, disputes can arise at this point because of philosophical differences among team members regarding mainstreaming and "inclusion." Keep in mind, the IDEA's LRE clause, along with any consistent state laws and regulations, and the body of judicial opinions interpreting this legislation in your jurisdiction, are the only legal guidance you have to decide the child's LRE.

Inclusion is a philosophy, backed up by various experts, techniques, and innovative proposals for delivering services, but it is not "the law." Nevertheless, inclusion philosophy has persuaded some judges to favor the mainstream, especially in cases involving young children who are free from disruptive behavior disorders or where the evidence shows the behavior disorders will respond to behavior management techniques that can be done in that setting. Even if your school runs a full inclusion program, remember that the IEP team still must have access to the full range of placement options contemplated in federal law in which to consider providing appropriate education. One or more IEP team members, at some point in the meeting after discussing the child's problem and the services needed to address it, should make a specific placement proposal or proposals to the team that is logically related to current assessment and the remediation of the problem. If this cannot be achieved, the meeting most likely should recess or adjourn and additional assessment be obtained as quickly as possible.

7. Exhausting All Options for Mainstreaming

Once the IEP team has agreed on services and the appropriate academic setting, the team should go back and reconsider other non-academic aspects of the child's program to make sure all available mainstreaming opportunities have been considered and exhausted. Dozens of non-academic activities take place in schools every day, and each presents an opportunity for every child to participate.

V. KEY DELIBERATIONS TO DOCUMENT

Any point worth serious discussion by the IEP team merits at least some passing mention in the written minutes of the team's deliberations. Any point that might be the subject of appeal to an impartial hearing officer certainly should be documented carefully. If the team's decisions are later disputed or appealed, the written record can help to establish what went on in the meeting, even if the key players have moved on to other positions, become unavailable for some other reason, or cannot independently remember what took place in the deliberations. Tape recording the team's deliberations may be a good idea in principle but in reality is rarely an adequate substitute for written minutes of deliberations. Recordings are often of poor quality, get lost or destroyed, or cannot be heard and understood because the team is engaging in lively debate and several people are talking at once. The written minutes of the team's deliberations thus should document all key points. Of particular importance, the team will want to ensure an unambiguous record of several essential points. The minimum information that should go into the written minutes of deliberations includes: (1) a summary of statements concerning the specific services that are deemed necessary by the team, as well as services about which team members disagree and a statement of the basis for disagreement; (2) a summary of statements concerning each specific setting that the committee considered "satisfactory" for implementing services and the basis of any disagreement regarding which settings would or would not be satisfactory; and (3) a summary of statements supporting the team's choice among the various settings where services might be implemented satisfactorily and reasons why the team rejected certain options.

VI. INVOKING STOP-GAP MEASURES

There is no way to overemphasize the importance to the IEP team of having current, relevant, and comprehensive information to support placement decisions and any other type of IEP decision. If the team members do not agree on the necessary types and amounts of services, it is possible they will not agree on the placement. If this happens, the best approach is to recess the meeting to obtain additional assessment or other input from professionals whose opinions on the disputed issue the parties are willing to take seriously. The background and training of those professionals, and the relevance of their findings and recommendations, will dictate how much weight the team ought to give to those findings and recommendations. For parents, this would be the point to consider requesting an independent educational evaluation from the school in the area where the dispute over services exists. The school's IEP team members should be able to point to some assessment that supports their proposal for services, and if the parent disagrees with that assessment, an IEE is the ticket. There are pros and cons of an IEE. Bringing in an outside agreed-upon expert usually means there will have to be compromise. Usually this is a good thing. It also means delay, however. For parents, the school officials may oppose the IEE, in which case there will be a due process hearing, with more delay, and the parent who presses ahead to obtain the outside assessment could be left holding the tab. Most of the time, however, school officials are willing to reimburse independent evaluations by qualified professionals whom all the team members respect. In any case, postponing the IEP meeting, or recessing the meeting when the lack of adequate information surfaces, usually means a better program for the child and a defensible IEP.

Chapter 4

THE IEP MEETING TO WRITE SPECIFIC GOALS AND OBJECTIVES

I. BACKGROUND

Goals and objectives have a vital place in the IEP process, because they address students' unique needs, relate those needs to an educational philosophy within our culture, and set the parameters for identifying the necessary services and placement. Transition goals embody parent and community preferences for the child's future after graduation. Selecting and drafting appropriate goals, objectives, and evaluation criteria taps expertise and creativity unique to special educators. It is an activity many find challenging and exciting. At the same time, objectives often can be written hurriedly, mechanically and without reference to assessment data, present performance, or what takes place in the classroom. This is unfortunate, because the writing of goals and objectives deserves as much attention as other, typically more controversial types of IEP decisions. This section suggests principles and strategies for the IEP team to approach this crucial task.

The Foundation: Proper Use of Assessment

Federal guidelines regarding the choice of goals and objectives is straightforward. The guidelines say, among other things, that goals and objectives should be written to address educational domains where the child's disability affects performance. This sounds simple enough but belies the complexity of how educators are to go about relating the disability to present performance deficits. Done properly, the current assessment is the starting point. The first step should be to examine the assessment to make sure the committee, particularly the parent, the

48

teacher, and staff who have not worked with the child before, has an understanding about the nature and severity of the child's disability and the areas of academic and non-academic performance that will be affected by the disability. If the assessment is out of date or if the assessment is current but circumstances have changed so that the child needs an update, it will be necessary to obtain this before proceeding.

The typical assessment of a learning disabled child illustrates limits of formal assessment. Federal guidelines and most states' laws require a significant discrepancy between actual and predicted academic performance in order establish special education eligibility. Most educators understand that assessment of cognitive and academic characteristics for determining eligibility must be based on a normative model, using tests designed to measure constructs rather than behaviors, and yield standard scores. While a test must be valid for its alleged purpose, the overriding components of validity have to do with the tests's internal psychometric properties with respect to its constructs, including score distributions, consistency, and reliability, with respect to different age groups and sub-populations. Most comprehensive assessments produce normative data necessary to understand the general dimensions of the child's problem and the severity of that problem when the child is compared to other children and to the child's own "predicted" scores. What's missing here, of course, is a description of the specific skills the child lacks right now, leading to school failure. That is the statement of present performance.

If the formal comprehensive assessment is current and accurate, the IEP team should take from it information about: (1) what aspect of the child's functioning (sensory, motor, cognitive, affective) is affected by the disability; (2) what specific scholastic and/or behavioral deficits are predicted based on assessment findings: and (3) what services are recommended in the assessment. The comprehensive assessment ordinarily will not give (for it is not designed to give) an up-to-date picture of what skills the child possesses today relative to the regular education curriculum or some other developmental framework of skills. Only a statement of present performance can do that.

Identifying Present Performance

Once the team has reviewed assessment to make sure all members understand the nature of the child's disability and the areas where the disability is expected to affect performance, the team needs to take a look at how the child is really functioning today. In other words, what skills does the child possess. Regulations say the statement of present performance must be written in objective, measurable terms. Further, there must be a direct relationship between the child's present performance and other components of the IEP. Thus, if the statement of present performance implies a problem in a certain area, such as the child's reading level, and points to a deficiency in a specific reading skill, then the IEP should address this deficiency with either aids and services in the mainstream, or special education, including goals, measurable objectives, special education instruction, and/or related services. The direct relationship should be evident from the child's present performance and the objectives themselves, or else the IEP team should explain the relationship in the minutes of deliberations.

It should be evident by now that it will not suffice to talk about standard scores or grade level functioning on a standardized test. For one thing, such measures will not support a convincing showing of progress. Further, they tend to invite the argument that for "progress" to occur the child must show a change in standard scores, which of course isn't necessarily true. Rather, the statement of present performance needs to reflect specific and measurable skills any professional could count or measure after reading the statement. The statement of present performance needs to be set down in the IEP, or else the IEP should reference some criterion-referenced or curriculum-referenced assessment data maintained in the child's records.

Surprisingly, the statement of present performance often is the most superficial part of the IEP. Teachers typically know a lot about the child's problem and how it affects learning, but rarely does that knowledge make it into the IEP, or for that matter anywhere else in records maintained by the school. There are different explanations for this omission. IEP team members sometimes behave as if they assume the eligibility, which is merely an administrative classification, is the disability itself and then let the discussion of eligibility pretermit inquiry into present performance. For autism, visual impairment, or deafness, the eligibility can be fairly descriptive of the underlying condition that causes a disability and the areas that will be affected by the disability. However, LD, TBI, OHI, and SED eligibilities encompass an array of syndromes causing different patterns of disability. If the child meets psychometric criteria for a math learning disability, shows abnormal scores on a measure of "depression," or had a severe head injury playing ball, the eligibility may be clear, but the IEP team still knows little about what the child can do and new skills the child needs to learn.

Unfortunately, the statement of present performance too often boils down to a cursory "below average in reading," "writes legibly at third grade level," or "exhibits disruptive behavior." If the IEP team writes a vague statement based mainly on psychometric findings, diagnostic impressions, or worse still the IDEA eligibility classification, then the team surely has glossed over the statement of present performance. This might not necessarily deny the child an appropriate education, where the disability is mild or circumscribed. However, it is certainly possible to achieve a sharper, verifiable understanding with measurable competencies, objectives and outcomes.

Ideally, the statement of present competencies should either detail the child's mastery of specific skills, or indicate a general summary of mastery and refer to documentation that provides the specifics. The IEP team must ultimately look to objectives stated in the regular curriculum or the child's last IEP and to the teacher's evaluative data including assignment sheets completed by the child, the child's responses on teacher tests, or other criterion referenced work product of the child. The teacher should be familiar enough with this material to supply written or oral evaluation data to the IEP team and should retain student made documentation for later proof.

So, after reviewing the assessment, the IEP team should carefully develop statements of present performance based on available data. These statements should be written in specific, objective, measurable terms. But what does this mean how specific should they be? From a lawyer's standpoint, which means from the standpoint of proving up student progress or failure under the IEP, the statement of present performance needs to be descriptive enough so that a teacher, parent, or hearing officer after reading the description could touch, see, hear, and count or measure the behavior in question.

Look at the statement of present performance from the last IEP you helped to write. Ask yourself, could a stranger reading that IEP at a later date understand what behaviors the IEP team was talking about why the IEP team chose a particular objective or whether the child's present performance is really different from last year's (hopefully because the child made progress)? If not, then it is likely your IEP team needs improvement in this area.

"Well," you might say, "all you have to do is look at the child's grades, or just ask the teacher if the child is making progress." This would be a good answer if grades could be tied to the achievement of specific skills, if teachers kept the child's work samples, remembered details about the child's work, and never changed jobs or moved out of town.

The most satisfying description of academic present competencies I have seen consisted of a lengthy, commercially-produced developmental checklist of specific measurable academic skills, organized generally by grade level and skill area (reading, language arts, math), with space set out to indicate the specific dates that: (1) instruction commenced on that skill; (2) the teacher most recently tested that skill; and (3) the child "mastered" the skill by meeting a criterion (usually, passing a test) set out in the curriculum. The checklist had places for the teacher to initial his or her recording of these dates. The child's present performance could be identified easily in this system just by referring to the skills that the child had already mastered. The current objectives would be those in progress, i.e. begun but not mastered, and the relationship between competencies and objectives is self-evident from the curriculum itself. The checklist could be attached to the IEP itself, establishing notice to all team members, with a fresh copy carried forward from year to year, supplemented with a new checklist to add each new grade-level's objectives. The teacher could forget, or move away, and it would still be possible to establish the child's progression.

Writing Goals and Objectives

IDEA still requires that the child's IEP have both long-term goals and near-term objectives. The statement of goals should reflect in general terms what the child is expected to accomplish over the duration of the IEP, usually one year. Goals need to be drawn from the statement of present performance and address the areas affected by the disability as reflected in the child's present performance. The IEP team's "expectation" for what the child will accomplish during the time period covered by the IEP rests on the team's understanding of the current assessment, including the type and severity of the disability. Goals should reflect an understanding of what the child is working toward, in order to either overcome or compensate for the disability.

In contrast, objectives are specific skills the observable, measurable steps and bench marks for teachers to address as part of reaching identified goals. The regulations state, somewhat differently, that short-term instructional objectives are measurable, intermediate steps between the child's present levels of educational performance and his or her annual goals. The objectives are developed based on a logical breakdown of the annual goals. Objectives tell teachers what to work on. Objectives are the heart of the IEP.

So, how does one write appropriate goals and objectives that directly relate to goals, present performance, and address areas of disability? One approach is to use some established framework, like a curriculum or developmental program, that identifies specific behavioral and cognitive skills, in domains affected by the disability, and orders those skills in a progression so that the acquisition of one set of skills (e.g. on a certain "grade level") becomes the foundation for selecting more advanced skills for example, using a checklist such as the one mentioned earlier. This curriculum should be backed up by specific assessment strategies that demonstrate "mastery" of each skill.

For non-disabled children and mainstreamed children with disabilities, the regular education curriculum usually serves this purpose. Of course, special education goals and objectives ordinarily will not be necessary for mainstreamed content areas. But even if the child is scheduled in special education and is not working on the chronologically appropriate grade level, the IEP team could still consider the regular curriculum at other levels as a source for appropriate academic goals and objectives. For other children with disabilities, a different developmental curriculum may be appropriate in academic and non academic domains affected by the disability.

The school district normally is free to choose curriculum so long as the curriculum has some support, in research or local usage, for adequately addressing skills affected by the disability. But no one would dispute that the choice of goals and objectives for an individual child with a disability is subject to IDEA's procedural safeguards. IEP team members occasionally disagree about the choice of goals and objectives because they disagree about the underlying curriculum, contending that the nature and/or sequence of objectives is inappropriate for the child's particular disability. One way to resolve this type of conflict is to retain an outside expert or panel of experts to study the situation and recommend one or more programs that are appropriate. If the school district elects to initiate or provoke litigation to defend a curriculum choice, the parties will usually end up paying for experts anyway, in addition to attorneys' fees. But the expense of litigation is a small risk when compared to the cost to the child of using an inappropriate curriculum just to avoid conflict within the team.

It is difficult to imagine that parents and school officials today would be unable to find a suitable, established curriculum with sequenced objectives, criteria, materials, and at least some research support, appropriate for use in most domains of functioning with most types of disability. More typically, educators have several curricula or developmental sequences to draw from in choosing appropriate goals and objectives. In any case, the overriding concerns, in either choosing among existing objectives or writing objectives unique to the child in question, are that objectives be: (1) observable and measurable, just as with the statement of present performance; (2) address areas affected by the disability as indicated from assessment and other indicia of present performance; (3) exist in a meaningful progression leading to more advanced objectives; and (4) move the child toward balanced, long-term annual goals and transition goals consistent with the child becoming an effective and productive member of society.

Evaluation

Current federal regulations say the IEP must include objective criteria, along with evaluation procedures and schedules, for determining whether the child is achieving short term objectives. Evaluation procedures and schedules should be included in the IEP. However, it is probably still true after reauthorization that it would be permissible to merely reference evaluation procedures in the IEP, so long as they exist somewhere the parent can access this information, and are clearly linked to short term objectives. The IEP team has to consider and approve the evaluation, and the choice of evaluation procedures and methods for a particular child is subject to IDEA procedural safeguards. Periodic evaluation of student progress toward goals and objectives must be provided to the parent on the same frequency as progress evaluations are provided to parents on non-disabled students.

Children with disabilities who are served in the mainstream with or without supplementary aids and services will experience regularly scheduled assignments, or examinations with or without modification, that serve as the basis for evaluating progress. Later on, the student's progress can be "proved up" with the student's exam itself, teacher grade books, work samples, assignments completed, and so on. Progress is summarized every six weeks, or some other grading period set under school board policy, and parents can expect at least that much feedback on how the child is doing.

Children with disabilities who are not educated in the mainstream still must undergo periodic evaluation. Parents are entitled to evaluative feedback that is at least as frequent and detailed as the school makes available for mainstreamed students. The special education program should have policy in place informing parents and teachers what frequency of evaluative feedback will be provided. Senate commentators on the new IDEA recommend an IEP "report card" to accompany the child's regluar education report card. Other students, however, may need more frequent evaluation and feedback, based on individual needs and learning characteristics. Procedures dictating the period for evaluating children in special education classes must be devised and communicated, through policy or through the IEP, not only to team members but also to all teachers who will participate in evaluating the child's work.

Once the periods for evaluating the child's progress are set, the mechanics of evaluating progress should be straightforward, so long as the IEP team has done a proper job of writing the statement of present performance, and the objectives, in observable and measurable terms. The task for evaluation is to observe and measure the skills scheduled for evaluation at the scheduled time. It goes without saying that the child's work product used for evaluation purposes should relate directly to, and test, the behaviors that manifest the specific objectives in the IEP. Tests and examinations that do not do this are inappropriate for evaluating the child.

II. WHAT DOCUMENTATION SHOULD THE TEAM HAVE AVAILABLE TO CONSIDER, AND WHY

1. The Most Recent Comprehensive Individual Assessment

As indicated, this will tell the IEP team the nature of the child's identified disability, and the predicted areas of academic deficiency caused by, or related to, that disability. If, in examining the child's present performance or other current teacher data, it appears the assessment does not predict the deficiencies that teachers are observing, an assessment update in any currently-observed deficiency area may be in order and should be discussed by the team.

2. The Most Recent IEP Documents

If the child has been receiving special education services based on a previously identified eligibility, the IEP team must examine the last IEP documents for the statement of present performance and the last set of goals and objectives. The team then must compare the scheduled objectives with the evaluation data before writing new goals and objectives for the upcoming IEP period. What the team should be doing with this information is comparing the child's last statement of present performance against the evaluation data for the last IEP's objectives to determine what progress the child made. The teacher should have test data, work-sheets, or other records to show how the child performs on tasks directly linked to stated objectives. If no progress can be established, the IEP team should consider whether further assessment is needed to help select more appropriate objectives, strategies, or supplementary aids and services.

3. Parent Records

The IEP team should consider any documentation the parent brings that is relevant to the selection or evaluation of goals and objectives. Typically, the complaint urged by many parents is their failure to understand what their child will be taught, based on reading objectives that are overly vague. Normally, this can be addressed simply by writing more specific objectives or by giving parents samples of test or work sheet material related to different objectives. However, parents sometimes bring reports or publications touting the latest advances for children with the disability in question and ask for the implementation of a specific curriculum or developmental model. Normally, the school district is responsible for choosing and implementing an appropriate curriculum or model, and thus the school's choice of approach should be given greater weight if supported by research and professional opinion and if the child's teachers can show that the child has been making progress. If the child is not making progress, the team needs hard data and opinions to show that the choice of objectives is not the problem. If that is not forthcoming, the team needs to look at all available models with appropriate objectives for the disability in question, and the specific support for each model found in research or competent professional judgment, before determining which is appropriate for choosing objectives for the child in question, based on the child's current assessment.

4. Teacher Records

Normally, the teacher has the most important information for the IEP team to consider in writing appropriate goals and objectives. If the student has not been in special education before, the regular education teacher's referral information and the child's work samples will establish present performance levels in areas affected by the disability. If the child has been in special education, the teacher's evaluative data from the last IEP will establish present performance for the current IEP team to use in selecting the appropriate new objectives. With present performance data in hand, the teacher should develop for the IEP team's consideration proposed objectives for the next year based on the child's learning characteristics and motivation.

5. Administrative Records

Records maintained by campus administrators may be of help to the committee in writing present performance descriptions, objectives, and evaluative data for social skill and other related objectives to address problem behaviors. Referral slips for conduct such as fighting, truancy, tardiness, skipping class, inappropriate language, and defiant or disruptive behavior often contain sufficient descriptive detail for assessment purposes. At least with behaviors occurring at greater frequency, counting the number of administrative referrals is one naturally-occurring data source for monitoring problem severity and response to interventions.

6. School Health Records

While educators rarely write IEP goals and objectives for health-related concerns, health records to a limited extent can inform the IEP team of factors that contribute to or exacerbate manifestations of a disability. Records of the child's visits to the school nurse also may offer insight where behavioral concerns from the classroom are related to illness, malingering, or stress - including stress caused by inappropriate goals and objectives.

7. Related Service Records

The focus of this discussion has emphasized educational, rather than related service goals and objectives primarily because related service assessment, goal setting, and evaluation usually require special expertise not available to most IEP team members. Therefore, IEP development for related services often is left substantially to the discretion of the related service provider. Nevertheless, the same considerations that apply to educational goals and objectives also apply to related services. The difference is mainly the specialized non-educational nature of the expertise required. From the standpoint of building a defensible IEP, this means if a dispute arises among team members regarding the type or amount of related service that is calculated to benefit the student, the issue of appropriateness has to be resolved in the end analysis by experts in that specialty area. The IEP team, of course, has discretion in selecting and timing the implementation of those particular IEP objectives that the related service supports. Related services do not exist in a vacuum from the rest of special education; rather, they are scheduled as necessary to enable the child to benefit from special education. In weighing educational priorities for a child at any given time, the team has to keep in mind that some learning objective, that the related services necessarily supports, must be written in the child's IEP so that there is a direct "relation" between that objective and the "related" service.

III. WHO SHOULD BE PRESENT AT THE IEP TEAM MEETING TO CONSIDER GOALS AND OBJECTIVES AND WHY?

1. The Parent

As with all IEP meetings, the parent should be present as the legal representative of the child and the person who, under IDEA, has the right to speak for the child's interests. With respect to the selection of goals and objectives, the parent ultimately should help the IEP team focus on teaching the child skills that the child will need to function at an independent, productive level in the community, consistent with the child's disability and potentials.

2. The Child's Special Education Teacher

If the child is currently in special education, this teacher brings essential evaluative data to the committee for the purpose of establishing present performance. Ideally the teacher will have evaluated the child on special education objectives, created a record of those evaluative data, and prepared for the team's consideration descriptive statements regarding the child's present performance on those objectives. The special education teacher also should be familiar with the current assessment, so that he or she can review areas of the child's functioning related to the disability, explain present performance in light of the disability, and recommend future objectives that logically follow the child's progression in the curriculum or developmental sequence. In cases where any of the child's regular education teachers cannot attend the meeting, the special education teacher should act as proxy, collecting and reporting information from those teachers.

3. The Child's Regular Education Teacher

If the child receives or may receive general education services, it is necessary that the child's regular education teacher attend the IEP team meeting to describe for the team the child's achievement with respect to mastering regular curriculum objectives and the child's classroom behaviors. The regular education teacher also is in a unique position to make recommendations to the team concerning the appropriateness of adding or deleting in the IEP specific supplementary aids and services for the regular classroom. If a general education teacher cannot attend the IEP team meeting, he or she should provide an oral or written summary of the relevant information to the special education teacher to present during the IEP team's deliberations.

4. A School Administrator

An administrator or someone designated by an administrator must attend the meeting as an official representative of the school district, empowered to commit the district's resources necessary for implementing the IEP. Often, the administrator also will have information relative to behavioral and social adjustment of the student that may be important to consider in developing goals and objectives for instruction or related services. The administrator as instructional leader may be the appropriate person to chair the IEP team.

5. The Child's Psychologist

If the child has a serious emotional disturbance or a behavior disorder related to a condition under a different eligibility (such as brain injury, ADHD, or excessive academic frustration), the IEP team should include or have input from the psychologist or other behavior specialist familiar with the child. This input should address the need for behavioral and social skill IEP objectives based on the child's present performance in classroom behavior and/or social skill domains.

6. Other Assessment Specialists

Other assessment specialists, including the providers of related services who assess the child in their area of expertise, must have input to the team in any areas affected by the disability where IEP goals and objectives are contemplated. A person must be present at the IEP team meeting who can interpret assessment results that are relevant to the team's deliberations.

4. THE ORDER OF BUSINESS FOR IEP TEAM MEMBERS

1. The Chairperson

The person who conducts the IEP team meeting to write annual IEP goals and objectives should be or should defer to someone with a working knowledge of the relationship between assessment, present performance, and writing objectives for the future. Often, this is a special education appraisal specialist or supervisor. This person needs to orchestrate the meeting to insure input from appraisal specialists, regular and special education teachers, and related service providers. This person also must be able to state assessment findings and teacher evaluation results in a manner comprehensible to parents who are not trained in education-related fields and create an atmosphere in which parent input is valued and carefully considered by other members of the team.

2. The Opening

The chair of the IEP meeting should begin by summarizing the purpose of the meeting, indicating that the team will review assessment and present performance, and write objectives for the upcoming year's IEP. The chair should review the proposed order of presentations, including the parent and/or the parent's representatives as well as the school district's representatives. The chair should inquire if the parent is satisfied with the notice received concerning the timing and content of the meeting, understands the order of business, and has any request to alter the agenda, raise additional issues for consideration, or present additional matter to the team.

3. Presenting Assessment Information and Identifying Present Performance

The IEP team must look over the current assessment, with special attention to those academic and nonacademic areas of the child's functioning that the assessment predicts will be affected by the disability. This is an important means of cross-checking the assessment against the overview of present performance, and vice versa. Often, if the team discovers a poor "fit" between what the assessment says the child should be doing in areas affected and what the child actually is doing, the team is alerted to the possible need for updated assessment. For example, if the last assessment indicates a learning disability affecting reading, but the child's present performance in reading is on grade level, and the child is showing severe disruptive behavior, then the current assessment is probably out of date even though it may not be three years old.

4. Identifying Present Performance

If the assessment appears current, the team should go on to elicit information from the child's teacher about the child's present performance in areas affected by the disability. It is essential here to review the evaluation of objectives scheduled in the previous annual IEP meeting, which the child (hopefully) has been working on. If the child is mainstreamed, receiving aids and services to address those areas, the team will need to hear from the regular teacher to determine if the child is mastering regular curriculum objectives and passing tests with the help of the aids and services.

If the Child Is Making Progress

If the child has made meaningful progress mastering special education objectives in the areas affected by the disability, then the team must write new objectives that build on the child's successes. If the mainstreamed child is mastering in the regular curriculum, the team will pass the child on to the next level.

If the Child Is Not Making Progress

If, however, the review of present performance indicates the child is not making meaningful progress on scheduled objectives, the team needs to explore the reason for this lack of progress and do something different in the next IEP to address the problem: write more appropriate objectives, increase services, alter instructional methods, or improve motivation. If the mainstreamed child is not progressing in the regular curriculum or shows an inability to participate in regular testing, the team's first task is to determine if the child is receiving sufficient and appropriate supplementary aids and services. If the team decides additional or different aids and services would improve performance in the mainstream setting, the team should schedule those aids and services. If the team thinks the child is receiving appropriate aids and services but still not progressing in an area affected by the disability, the team should consider providing special education in that area, either in the regular classroom or in some different appropriate setting that is the least restrictive environment.

5. Choosing Goals and Objectives

If the child has succeeded in mastering the objectives scheduled in the previous IEP, this gives the team a strong indication that the goals, as well as the curriculum or developmental progression the school has chosen, are appropriate to address the disability. The team will want to write new developmentally appropriate goals for the next year that build on last year's mastery, or if the child is mainstreamed, continue the child at the next level in the regular curriculum. If the child's success in special education has enabled the child to master some or all of the skills of the regular curriculum at the child's grade level, the team will need to consider whether mainstream placement with aids and services would allow the child to continue making meaningful progress in the less restrictive setting.

6. Identifying Evaluation Procedures

Once goals and objectives are selected, the team must indicate in the IEP, at least in general terms, the type and frequency of evaluation methods to determine progress on those objectives. Specific evaluation methods should be reflected in the school's records, accessible to the parent, and special education teachers should retain sufficient documentation of the child's work, in the way of test responses, work sheets, or completed assignments, to prove that the child has mastered or failed to master special education objectives. A special education teacher also should be responsible for making contact with the child's regular education teacher to insure adequate documentation of the child's progress in mainstream classes.

V. KEY DELIBERATIONS TO DOCUMENT

Any point that is worth serious discussion by the IEP team deserves mention in the written minutes of the team's deliberations. This is particularly true if the point is disputed or may be the subject of an appeal. If the team's decisions are questioned in a due process hearing, the written record can help to establish what the team discussed in the meeting even if the members later become unavailable or cannot remember what took place. Of particular importance, the team will want to ensure an unambiguous record of several essential points. (1) Document what current assessment shows to be the expected areas of disability and how severe is the disability. State whether team members agree or disagree about the assessment and any assessment findings that are disputed. Indicate whether further assessment is necessary because the last assessment is no longer accurate. (3) State the child's present performance in areas affected by the disability. If information about specific skills is not detailed in the IEP itself, indicate where this information may be found for inspection. State what evaluative data the IEP team used to establish performance on past objectives and identify present performance. (4) Describe how present performance data compares with the last IEP and indicate whether the child is, or is not, making progress on objectives in the areas affected by the disability. If the child is not making progress, summarize what the team believes to be the problem. Indicate if further assessment is necessary to identify the problem and what questions the assessment is to answer. (5) If the child made progress under the old IEP, the team needs to draft and include in the written IEP goals and measurable objectives for the next year or other period covered by the IEP. (6) Describe, either in general or specific terms, what evaluation of current objectives will be done and when.

VI. INVOKING STOP-GAP MEASURES

As with any other type of IEP team dispute, the team may recess the discipline IEP meeting, as mentioned in the preceding discussion of IDEA procedural options, at any point the team feels further assessment is needed, or additional documentation or references need to be reviewed, or outside persons need to be consulted or perhaps invited to be part of the team, or merely because tensions need time to wind down. Often a recess, possibly coupled with informal alternative dispute resolution, allows the team members who are in disagreement to find alternatives that will resolve the impasse and produce an acceptable solution, as well as an appropriate IEP for the child.

Chapter 5

THE IEP MEETING TO WRITE THE BEHAVIOR MANAGEMENT PLAN

I. BACKGROUND

New IDEA requirements place special emphasis on behavior management by requiring a behavioral assessment or review of behavior management for a child with a disability whenever the child is referred for disciplinary action. A behavior management plan, or BMP, usually consists of a set of procedures aimed at increasing or decreasing specified behaviors that affect the child's ability to participate in instruction. The BMP does two things: it supersedes and modifies the classroom and administrative consequences that ordinarily would apply to the behavior covered by the BMP; and it applies techniques which, based on research and/or competent professional judgment, are reasonably calculated to improve behavior. The BMP can be delivered either as special education, if implemented as part of special education, or as supplementary aids and services, if implemented in the regular classroom to support mainstreaming. Either way, the BMP ordinarily applies to all staff who interact with the child covered by the BMP because the BMP usually must be applied consistently.

If a child's disability affects his or her emotional and behavioral functioning, as, for example, when the child has a condition leading to special education eligibility of serious emotional disturbance, autism, or other health impairment based on ADHD, the IEP team should tend to assume the child's need for a BMP. These conditions, by their nature, imply behavioral manifestations that interfere with instruction. It is also true that many disabling conditions can cause behavioral deficits or excesses that interfere with instruction, even if those conditions do not lend themselves to eligibility under the emotional disturbance classification. In such a case, disability-related behaviors could lead to disciplinary consequences and require specialized behavioral interventions other than regular discipline. The questions for the IEP team concern whether the child's condition of disability causes or affects the child's behavioral excesses or deficits and whether behaviors will respond to manipulation of the antecedents or consequences in school, or at home if the disability necessitates in-home training and/or parent training.

At the same time, it is also true that no particular eligibility is a legal prerequisite to writing a BMP. IDEA now requires that students with disabilities who receive certain types of disciplinary removal also are given a functional assessment, or reassessment, of the behavior that caused the disciplinary removal. This requirement is not limited to students with emotional and behavioral disabilities. Therefore, the functional assessment must address even behaviors that are not suspected of being related to any disability. The assessment may, of course, conclude that regular discipline consequences are appropriate to address the behavior or the assessment may recommend some modification of regular disciplinary consequences to address disability-related issues.

New federal regulations and case law should help to clarify the extent of the school's responsibility to address behaviors of eligible students that are unrelated to the child's disability. But, how "directly" must a behavior relate to the disability before the school becomes obligated to modify the normal classroom or administrative disciplinary consequences for that behavior by writing a BMP to address the behavior? There is no definitive legal answer to this question at present. Legal precedents from cases involving disciplinary expulsion of disabled students suggest that the relationship or "manifestation" must be both direct and causal. However, the authors have yet to find a definitive court opinion that applies this "direct and causal" standard to the issue of whether the school could refuse to write a BMP for a disabled student who misbehaves, because the behavior was not related to the disability in a direct and causal way. New IDEA mandates may further complicate this issue. Teachers know that students with learning disabilities experience and act out classroom frustrations that are indirectly "caused" by the learning disability, even though the behavior may not result directly from the child's inability to read and solve math problems. Children with traumatic brain injury may exhibit behavioral disturbances that physicians cannot say to a medical certainty are "caused" by the brain injury, though they may suspect a causal relationship. Does IDEA *require* BMPs for such children, even if the child can otherwise receive regular discipline because the behavior was not a manifestation of the child's inability to read and solve math problems? Until such questions are answered, if they are ever answered, IEP teams have to rely on the best available professional expertise from persons with training and experience in the disability in when they select behaviors for regular discipline modification, special education intervention, or supplementary aids and services.

For a child who is not in a specialized behavior classroom or unit with a comprehensive behavior management system as a matter of policy, the BMP ordinarily will be a part of the child's IEP so that staff who interact with the child will be given notice that the BMP must be implemented. Even children in specialized programs still may require a BMP with individualized consequences, depending on the nature of their disability, the characteristics of the program, and the extent to which the child is mainstreamed or otherwise served in different settings. But every child who needs special education to address problem behavior also requires individualized specific behavioral objectives in the IEP. That is, for a child whose behaviors interfere with instruction, the IEP should contain objectives to address behavioral excesses or deficits affected by the disability. These objectives should address the appropriate behaviors the child needs to exhibit to be successful behaviors that, according to assessment and the statement of present performance, the child is not exhibiting. Preferably, behavior IEP objectives will be stated in positive terms. They should describe appropriate "replacement" behaviors that would lead to success, if substituted for the inappropriate behavior excesses or deficits causing a problem. In the structuring of the child's IEP, the statement of present performance describes the current behavior problems, and the behavior goals and objectives indicate the competencies that the child is working toward. The BMP, then, contains the specific procedures for modifying existing antecedents and consequences of the behavior, calculated to decrease disruptive or self-defeating behaviors that interfere with instruction, and to increase positive replacement behaviors.

The reader is urged to review the chapter on writing goals and objectives before planning the IEP team meeting to address behavior management.

Reviewing Current Assessment

In dealing with behavior management, as with other IEP issues, the IEP team first looks at the presenting problem behaviors in the context of current assessment. The first question is whether, given the nature and severity of the disability, the problem behavior is affected by or, in different phraseology, is a manifestation of, the disability. The next question is, what changes to existing antecedents and consequences in the school environment would likely decrease the problem behavior and increase appropriate replacement behavior. If the child has an existing eligibility of serious emotional disturbance, the current assessment should address these questions directly and should be the starting point for deliberations. If the child has some other eligibility, the team should consider whether the behavior is mainly affected by that disability or whether the team suspects that the child has some other disability and thus requires further assessment of that suspected disability. Regardless of the eligibility, however, the team needs qualified professional opinion that answers these two crucial questions before the team can proceed. If for any reason the current assessment is not helpful in addressing these questions, then the team should obtain further assessment from a qualified psychologist and/or behavior management specialist.

Identifying Present Performance the Baseline

Once the team has reviewed assessment to make sure all members understand the nature of the child's disability and the manner in which the disability is expected to affect behavior and emotional adjustment, the team must develop an accurate description of the child's current functioning in observable, measurable terms. This statement should clearly and dispassionately reflect the behaviors that cause trouble for the child and others, including the situations where they typically occur, and also should describe behavioral strengths of the child and where the child is able to exhibit those strengths.

Describing theoretical constructs about the child's underlying disorder, using terms such as "depressed," "anxious," or "socially maladjusted," may be essential at the assessment stage. However, such descriptions have no place at the stage of identifying present performance. These terms are simply too general to be of use in school programming and may cause more confusion in the efforts of school staff. The statement of present performance needs to address observable behaviors, including verbal statements, nonverbal statements, cognitive problem-solving characteristics, and or behavior excesses and deficits of the child, that staff can begin to evaluate and work with. The statement of present performance should either stand alone as the "baseline" for subsequent behavioral programming or should point directly to other data in the child's record that will serve as the measurable baseline.

At this stage many IEP team members will be feeling frustrated about the child's misbehavior, often the child's most prominent and visible characteristic, and neglect to include the child's positive behavioral and social competencies in the statement of present performance. This skewed view of the child, if it becomes enshrined in the IEP documentation, causes three typical problems for the IEP team later down the road. First, it fails to emphasize the adaptive behaviors that already exist, which teachers should be building on and strengthening to replace maladaptive behaviors. Second, it makes the team's statement of present performance inaccurate, which later could lead an observer to call in question the accuracy of other conclusions of the IEP team. Finally, it makes the child's disability sound more severe than it really is, so that the IEP services the team schedules, even though sufficient to address the problem's real severity, will seem inadequate and thus make the IEP appear flawed to an observer who is not familiar with the underlying facts.

Existing regulations say the statement of present performance must be written in objective, measurable terms and must relate directly and logically to other IEP components such as objectives, services, and placement. If the statement of present performance indicates a behavioral or emotional problem that is affected by the child's disability, then the IEP must address this problem with either aids and services in the mainstream, or special education, including goals, measurable objectives, special education instruction, and/or related services. The relationship between behavioral deficiencies identified in the statement of present performance, and the objectives and services in the IEP, should be self-evident from the statement of present performance and the objectives and services themselves, or else the IEP team should explain the relationship in the minutes of deliberations.

Writing Behavior Objectives

Without behavioral IEP objectives, the behavior management plan is like a rudderless ship steaming in circles. It seems, nevertheless, that

BMPs often address only inappropriate behaviors and their consequences. The teacher and the student thus spend their time focusing on what the child is *not* to do and are left without clear direction about what it is the child *is* to do. This is particularly true with mainstreamed children who lack the normal repertoire of organizational and study skills at independent level of mastery, and children lacking appropriate role models of behaviors for dealing with authority figures and peers. Teachers cannot simply consequate these children's inappropriate behaviors and then sit back and expect learning to take its course. Yet, teachers without background dealing with emotionally disturbed children often do just this for want of training and support. The place to start providing this support is in the IEP statement of goals and objectives. Behavior problems require clear, objective, measurable goals, as do other kinds of learning problems affected by the child's disability. If the IEP team devotes the same attention and follows the same process for behavior goals as for instructional goals, then the BMP will reflect this by identifying and providing consequences for adaptive behaviors as well as for inappropriate behaviors.

The Behavior Management Plan

Once the team has reviewed the assessment and written the statement of present performance, including a clear, objective, and measurable statement describing not only the problem behavior but also the appropriate replacement behavior or behaviors, then the team is ready to write the BMP. Recall that the BMP has two major purposes, and the IEP team must address both. One purpose is to provide a substitute for all or some of the administrative consequences that otherwise would befall the child, if the child's misbehavior were not affected by the child's disability. The other purpose is to make a plan that, according to research and/or the opinion of an appropriately trained professional, will eliminate or decrease the misbehavior and teach the child some other, more acceptable alternative means of self-expression.

"Spare the rod, and spoil the child" is a saying that expresses the discipline philosophy of many schools. That punishment-oriented philosophy prevails because the threat of punishment is effective for most misbehavior of most children. These children come to school already having acquired or developed critical psychological attributes conducive to self-control, orienting to learning tasks, and responding to authority. Once in school, they become caught up in the excitement of learning and discovery. For these children, the abstract threat of having a conference with the vice-principal, getting "swats," being banished to detention hall, or being suspended from school is enough to curb most impulses to break school rules.

Obviously many other children, those whose disabilities affect their behaviors and emotional responses in school and who lack a foundation of learning skills, do not respond in the conventional way to conventional discipline. Or they respond appropriately to some conventional discipline strategies but not to others. For these children, the IEP team's task is to identify the consequences provided under regular discipline policy that are likely to be effective, that is, to decrease or inhibit the child's unacceptable disability-related behaviors. The team then must distinguish which consequences will not be effective. Once this has been done, the team will write the IEP to modify the normal course of school discipline, for the child and the behavior in question, so that there is no misunderstanding about which consequences are available to use and which are not.

The team's other task is to develop a schedule of consequences for decreasing misbehavior and substituting appropriate behavior. "Schedule" in this context means the specific "when and how" of the BMP, as well as the "what." The team has approximately two ways to go at this stage. One way is to write a "checklist" BMP that simply selects, from a menu of options, those techniques that the team thinks will help the teacher to change the child's behaviors. This type of BMP contains the "what" and leaves the "when and how" up to the teacher's discretion. Obviously a checklist BMP has to be backed up by more extensive documentation, and in-service training, to explain the meaning of the various menu options for teachers. The checklist BMP gives the teacher latitude in applying the various options that the team has selected from the menu which clearly requires that the teacher already has some professional training in behavior management, reads the checklist, and understands the various options.

There are pros and cons to using checklist BMPs. Some school attorneys say they should never be used. Frankly, that is the safest advice, if you are making no presumption regarding the child's educational need or if you are unwilling to take steps to support the checklist with necessary documentation and teacher training. But the BMP checklist also can be a time-efficient tool under certain circumstances. These circimstances may include the following. First, the district must have, and must distribute to teachers, a handbook or manual describing in practical terms what each item in the menu of options means in terms of teacher behavior. Second, the options should be limited to basic, well-researched, and relatively uncontroversial management techniques such as increased positive reinforcement, time-out, special rewards, use of points or other tangible rewards, etc. Third, the district must document that it has provided in-service training on the use of those options to any teacher who will be using those options. Fourth, the school must limit the use of the "checklist" BMP to children whose behavior problems are not severe. This normally would include children who are not seriously emotionally disturbed but whose disability-related behaviors interfere with instruction and will not respond to normal school discipline. The checklist is most useful for children whose only needed behavior management strategy involves relieving the student from normal disciplinary consequences.

Take, for example, the child experiencing mild anxiety or depression triggered by stress from having to cope with a learning disability. The child's productivity is affected. She is not finishing assignments on time. Assume the school's discipline policy ordinarily requires children to attend a detention hall as the consequence for turning assignments in late. The IEP team feels, however, that detention hall would only increase this child's stress by singling her out and exposing her to peer taunting and possibly increase her work inhibition. The team might very reasonably assume that a different consequence, such as a visit to the counselor instead of detention hall, would be more likely to get the student through this temporary disability-related turmoil. In that case, the child does not require a highly specific, detailed, and structured BMP. She needs a simple directive from the IEP team to the teacher possibly in the form of an appropriately marked checklist indicating that detention hall is not an option for late assignments but referral to the counselor is. The team could write all that information out by hand, but the checklist, if supported by proper interpretive manuals and teacher training, is faster to use and potentially more standardized in its application. The words are the same every time, and the team does not need to expend further effort making sure each and every teacher gets training in the meaning of this particular BMP.

Contrast this with the second example. Our second child is eligible for special education because of serious emotional disturbance based on depression and atypical psychosis. Usually he can attend to task and respond to teacher directives early in the day, but later on he becomes agitated, wandering around the room pulling off his clothing and touching other children or their materials, quickly escalating to a panic state in which he talks to imaginary people, tries to hit or cut himself, and strikes out at teachers or other children who try to help him. A checklist BMP for this child will not be sufficient. This child requires a very specific, detailed, and highly individualized program going well beyond what can be conveyed in a standardized format like a checklist even one backed by extensive training materials.

This second example leads to a discussion of the second approach to writing BMPs. This approach contains the true "schedule" for specifically modifying antecedents and consequences to deal with more severe behavior problems. Here, the BMP needs to specify exactly what behaviors, and under what circumstances, trigger what consequences. Often, this type of BMP requires writing a script telling every teacher exactly what to say and what to do, in response to each behavior in the child's typical escalating sequence of behaviors. No simple checklist can ever hope to approach the degree of specificity, planfulness, and individual accommodation required by children with more severe emotional and behavior disorders.

Very often, these children with more severe emotional and behavioral disorders will have several professionals working with the child and family, professionals in the school as well as in outside clinics or community agencies. Sometimes, these children will be prescribed psychoactive medications. Sometimes they will have several diagnoses implicating not only emotional disorders but also neurological and developmental conditions as well. The complexity of these cases belies the appropriateness of a checklist and clearly calls for a highly specific and individualized team approach. The IEP team must solicit input from all the outside professionals treating the child regarding recommendations for appropriate interventions. The team must understand what behaviors are likely to respond to modifications in the environment in school, i.e. the BMP, and what if any behaviors are more likely to respond to other interventions such as medication.

With this information in hand, the team still has many variables to consider before writing the BMP. For example, can the child respond to delayed rewards, or are frequent specific feedback and consequences necessary? If the child needs frequent feedback, would it be helpful to give verbal praise, points or tokens, or does the child only respond to tangible rewards? When should the child be allowed to exchange points or token reinforcement and for what menu of consequences? Can the child process verbal instructions, or are modeling and gestural communication needed to teach appropriate behaviors? Can the child sequence several behaviors in a complex chain, or should reinforcement be directed at limited specific component behaviors? Does the child have strong emotional reactions that it interfere with reality testing at some times but not at others, and if so, how should teachers respond to these reactions? Will the child require physical restraint or emergency medication, and if so, how are these consequences to be delivered? These sorts of questions will need to be answered, by school experts or outside professionals before proceeding to draft the objectives and the schedule of consequences.

Normally, the most important facet of a behavior management plan is its comprehensiveness. A well-designed plan is one that addresses all possible options and provides clear guidance to the staff regarding how to respond to each behavior expected of the child. For more severe disorders, the plan assumes the presence of adequate staff who are trained and experienced in managing behavior crises quickly and calmly. Usually, turmoil and disruption among staff and other children only reinforces and/or escalates the disruptive child's behavior. Therefore, having a simple and effective plan, and well-trained staff, are of the utmost importance.

The child's placement must have sufficient staff support to insure that BMP consequences are applied as written for every occurrence of the behavior, or as close as humanly possible. This means the discussion of BMP issues often will lead to a discussion of LRE for the child. IEP team members need to be aware of this and be prepared to discuss and analyze the various placement options under the applicable LRE standard. Many campuses are now supporting mainstreaming efforts by making teams of behavior specialists available to support the regular classroom teacher as needed managing child behaviors. Other schools implement "level" systems serving the child with a disability in a restrictive, highly structured behavior management classroom but only as long as it takes for the child to get control of the disruptive behavior. The point is that, perhaps more than any other subgroup, children with emotional and behavioral disabilities require consideration of the full continuum of options for effective placement.

Evaluation

Existing federal regulations and new IDEA requirements say the IEP must include objective evaluation criteria, along with evaluation procedures and schedules, for determining, on at least an annual basis, whether the child is achieving short-term objectives. Furthermore, evaluation procedures must track progress during the school year so that the parent can have something like a regular report card showing how far the child has moved toward the annual goal during the reporting period. Children with behavioral and emotional disabilities serious enough to require an individualized BMP also require individualized evaluation procedures linked to the BMP. If behavior IEP objectives are written properly and inappropriate behaviors also detailed in objective, measurable terms, evaluation should be straightforward. Ordinarily, counting or otherwise documenting behaviors is intrinsic to behavioral methodology and thus dovetails with IDEA's IEP evaluation requirements.

II. WHAT DOCUMENTATION SHOULD THE TEAM HAVE AVAILABLE TO CONSIDER AND WHY?

1. The Most Recent Comprehensive Individual Assessment

As is true with respect to writing goals and objectives, the assessment tells the IEP team the nature of the child's identified disability and the domains the team should expect will be affected by that disability. If the assessment causes the team to expect behavioral deficits, the team then needs to examine the child's present performance to determine whether this expectation is borne out. If the child's present performance does not reflect problems in the behavioral domain, or at least problems affecting the child's functioning in school, then the team needs to decide whether it will be necessary to update the assessment in emotional and behavioral domains before the team can plan IEP goals, objectives, and services. If more assessment is needed, the team should schedule objectives and strategies based on the best available professional input to the team and revisit the IEP when the assessment update is completed. At whatever point the team is satisfied that the child's assessment is current and accurate, the team will be able to verify the nature of the disability and the domains affected by that disability. If emotional and/or behavioral domains are affected and present performance indicates an ongoing problem, the team will need to consider appropriate objectives and strategies, including a BMP.

2. The Most Recent IEP Documents

If the child has been receiving special education services, the IEP team should review the statement of present performance and the goals and objectives from the last IEP in emotional and behavioral domains. The team should then determine what progress has been made by comparing current evaluation data against the last set of objectives. The school often will have readily available evaluative data from BMP point sheets, frequency counts, administrative referrals, and other data sources. If, after examining these data sources, the IEP team is unable to establish that the child is making progress or is able to establish that the child is not making progress, the team should revisit the child's IEP objectives and strategies, including BMP, for indications that the objectives, the strategies, or both objectives and strategies, are not appropriate. If the team determines that the child is making progress, the team should identify the effective components of the IEP and take care to incorporate those components into the strategies that may be needed for the IEP that is being written.

3. Parent Records

The IEP team should consider any documentation the parent brings that is relevant to the selection and evaluation of goals, objectives, and strategies in the emotional and/or behavioral domains. Here, several types of parent input will be important. Records documenting non-school stresses that might affect the child's symptomatic in-school behavior help the team interpret the meaning of such behavior and select appropriate strategies. Parents desiring privacy often obtain outside consultation from mental health providers. Given the potential importance of this information to understanding in-school problems, school representatives should invite and encourage parents to share relevant reports with the IEP team or invite outside providers to present their information to the team in person. School representatives should explain the extensive protections available to safeguard the confidentiality of educational records without overlooking the exceptions to confidentiality.

4. Teacher Records

The child's regular and/or special education teachers usually have critical documentation regarding the child's emotional and behavioral functioning. Although teachers may not feel qualified to make mental health assessments, their intuitive perceptions of the nature and meaning of a child's adjustment, contained in anecdotal notes and records, usually gives the IEP team and mental health professionals valuable data for understanding the issues. They see firsthand the child's typical reactions to stress, success, failure, and peer interactions both positive and negative. Frequently, teachers have documentation concerning the child's functioning in the community. If the child has an IEP with behavior objectives and evaluation, the teacher usually will be the person to create and maintain evaluative data. If the child does not have behavior objectives, the teacher usually will have created and maintained some notes, logs, and other records of observations that shed light on behavior problems. This information is essential to develop the statement of present performance and to write and prioritize behavior objectives and strategies.

5. Administrative Records

Records created or maintained by campus administrators can be valuable to develop the statement of present performance in the emotional and behavioral domain. Often, administrators will have dealt extensively with a child's problem behaviors, by way of teacher referrals for discipline or counseling, long before any specialized strategies are written. Because of prior training and experience, or just having to deal with many different campus crises, many administrators have good insight into children's adjustment problems, and their logs and notes reflect this. Administrative referral records for misconduct incidents that violate the campus discipline code often contain a great deal of descriptive information and are a naturally occurring data source for evaluating the severity of behavior problems and their response to IEP interventions, at least with respect to the kinds of behavior problems that recur frequently.

6. School Health Records

Health records may aid the IEP team in understanding the causes and dynamics of behavior problems affected by a disability. For example, children's affective problems or excessive anxiety often appear first in the form of somatic complaints leading to referrals to the school nurse, who typically finds no evidence of a physical problem. Emotional and behavioral problems can be exacerbated by illness or other physical problems, to the extent that interferes with the workings of educational and behavioral interventions. Educators need to avoid misinterpreting temporary fluctuations in behavior evaluative data that are caused by physical problems rather than the inappropriateness of the IEP. And physical problems such as TBI, seizure disorders, and other neurological conditions directly affect emotional and behavioral functioning. The school's health professionals or some other appropriately qualified member of the IEP team must review and interpret health information, for purposes of updating assessment (if necessary), describing present performance, and designing appropriate objectives and strategies.

7. Related Service Records

Students with disabilities affecting the emotional and behavioral domain obviously can have a variety of underlying conditions needing a variety of services. Students with psychological problems, for example, sometimes have counseling as a related service as necessary to address attitudes, feelings, and social skills related to objectives in the appropriate domain. Students with neurological problems may require occupational therapy as a related service to address psychomotor and/or organizational skills directly affecting behavior. The IEP team should consider the records and other input of related service providers in developing the statement of the child's present performance. Those records may indicate both problem areas and strengths useful in crafting appropriate objectives, designing strategies and, if appropriate, involving the related service directly in the behavior management plan.

III. WHO SHOULD BE PRESENT AT THE IEP TEAM MEETING TO WRITE THE BEHAVIOR MANAGEMENT PLAN AND WHY?

1. The Parent

As with all IEP meetings, the parent should be present as the legal representative of the child and the person who, under IDEA, has the right to speak for the child's interests. With respect to the selection of behavior goals, objectives, and strategies, parent input should help to address the historical and noneducational influences on the child's behavior, the professional opinions of any outside experts who have worked with the child, and the parent's own experience regarding what strategies and consequences are effective in dealing with the child's behavior in non-school settings. Parent cooperation may be critical in implementing some types of behavior management plans, particularly with younger children for whom in-home consequences may be more salient than consequences in school, and children with severe behavioral disabilities who require consistency across different settings in order to control and shape behavior. The team must elicit parent input to insure that the parent understands behavioral strategies that usually are described in the IEP with "buzz words" like reinforcement, extinction, time out, CPI or crisis intervention, life space interview, and the like.

2. The Child's Special Education Teacher

If the child is currently in special education, this teacher has essential evaluative data for establishing present performance in the emotional and behavioral domain. If the child does not have behavior management strategies in place in the existing IEP, the special education teacher very likely will have been consulted as behavior problems developed and have direct knowledge from observing the child. If the child already has a BMP in place, the special education teacher often is the person designated to collect and summarize behavioral data to help the team evaluate the effectiveness of the plan's strategies. The special education teacher thus should have some record of contact with the child and some opinions supported by training and experience regarding the behaviors in question. The special education teacher also should be familiar with the current assessment to help review the child's functioning in areas related to the disability, explain present performance in light of the disability, and recommend future objectives from a background of knowledge regarding children's social and emotional development. If the child's regular education teacher cannot attend the meeting, the special education teacher should be the person to collect and report information from regular education.

3. The Child's Regular Education Teacher

If the child receives or may receive regular education services, the child's regular education teacher must attend the IEP team meeting to describe the child's classroom behaviors, social skills, and emotional adjustment. The regular education teacher is the only person who can tell the IEP team what supplementary aids and services are necessary to accommodate the child's behavioral disability in the regular classroom. If the regular education teacher cannot attend the IEP team meeting, he or she should provide an oral or written summary of the relevant information to the special education teacher to present during the IEP team's deliberations.

4. A School Administrator

An administrator or someone designated by the school administration must attend the IEP team meeting as an official representative of the school district, empowered to commit the district's resources necessary for implementing the IEP. Often, the administrator will have information relative to the child's behavior, as well as family and community circumstances, that are important to consider in developing behavior goals, objectives, and strategies.

5. The Child's Psychologist

For the child who has disability affecting the emotional and behavioral domain, such as a psychological or psychiatric disorder, brain injury, ADHD, or even learning disability with excessive academic frustration, the IEP team should include as a member, or have input from, the school's psychologist or other behavior specialist familiar with the child. This input should address the need for behavioral and social skill IEP objectives based on the child's present performance in classroom behavior and/or social skill domains. The psychologist also should address the appropriateness of strategies to include in the BMP to address the child's disability-related behaviors.

6. Other Assessment Specialists

Other specialists, including the providers of related services, should have input to the team regarding objectives and strategies to address emotional and behavioral disabilities that affect behavior, to the extent of their background of training and experience relevant to the child's disabilities. A person must be present at the IEP team meeting who can interpret assessment results that are relevant to the team's deliberations.

IV. THE ORDER OF BUSINESS FOR IEP TEAM MEMBERS

1. The Chairperson

In the IEP team meeting to address behavior management, the person who runs the IEP team meeting should have a general working knowledge of the interrelationship between assessment, present performance, and the choice of emotional and behavioral objectives. The conditions that give rise to emotional and behavioral disabilities are so numerous and diverse that the chair ought to have some background of training and/or experience with behavioral disabilities. Often, the chair will need to be a special education coordinator, appraisal specialist, or supervisor. This person needs to insure input from appraisal specialists, regular and special education teachers, and related service providers. This person must be sensitive to assure that assessment findings and IEP evaluation results are explained so that participants can understand.

2. The Opening

The chair of the IEP meeting should begin by summarizing the purpose of the meeting, indicating that the team will review assessment, review present performance, and decide on appropriate behavioral objectives and strategies for the upcoming year's IEP. The chair should review the proposed order of presentations, including the parent and/or the parent's representatives as well as the school district's representatives. The chair should inquire if the parent is satisfied with the notice received concerning the timing and content of the meeting and understands the order of business, the agenda of items for discussion, and the parent's rights under IDEA and state law. The chair should ask if the parent would like to request a change in the agenda for the meeting. Regardless of whether the school or the parent scheduled the IEP meeting, the chair should ask whether the parent wishes to raise any particular issue for discussion or add to the issues already scheduled for consideration.

3. Presenting Assessment Information and Identifying Present Performance

The IEP team must review current assessment, in order to understand emotional and behavioral characteristics that the assessment says will be affected by the disability. As with other IEP issues, this step allows the team to check the assessment against the child's present performance, and vice versa. If the team discovers a poor "fit" between what the assessment predicts and what the child actually is doing, the team should consider the need for updated assessment. For example, if the last assessment indicates that the child has characteristics of a conduct or antisocial disorder but the child today is exhibiting sad mood, lack of initiative, and crying spells, the team might have cause to question the accuracy of the assessment and consider updating it.

4. Identifying Present Performance

Once the team is satisfied that the assessment is current and sufficiently accurate to rely on in identifying the characteristics of the disability, including the emotional and behavioral domains affected by the disability, the team should elicit information from the child's teacher about the child's present performance in those domains. In the process of doing that, the team must review the evaluation of any prior objectives that the child has been working on in the affected emotional and behavioral domains. If there are no such objectives, then the team should describe the child's present performance in terms of "baseline" behavioral or other data collected up to the time of the IEP meeting to address the behavioral or emotional problem. At this point the team should be ready to address emotional and behavioral goals and objectives and strategies. The input of the classroom teacher, the psychologist, and/or the behavior specialist should drive this portion of the deliberations with input from other team members as needed.

If the Child Is Making Progress

If the child already has emotional and/or behavioral objectives, and is making meaningful progress on those objectives then the team must write new objectives that build on the child's successes. This requires input from the teacher and any team members with special expertise regarding emotional and behavioral development.

If the Child Is Not Making Progress

If the child already has emotional and behavioral objectives but is not making meaningful progress on those objectives, the team needs to explore the reason for this lack of progress and either choose more appropriate objectives, change or increase services, revise the behavior management plan, if any, or all of the foregoing. As in the case of IEP services in other instructional domains, if the child is mainstreamed and the team decides additional or different services are necessary to enable the child to make progress, the team will need to review the placement options and assess whether the mainstream remains the LRE for the child. If the team is unable to reach consensus on the cause and remediation of the child' failure to progress, with the expertise and resources available at the time of the IEP meeting, the team should call in additional expertise and, if necessary recess to obtain more information and/or assessment.

5. Choosing Goals and Objectives

If the child has succeeded with emotional and behavioral objectives from the previous IEP, the team obviously must give strong consideration to building incrementally on the current theory or model of the child's disability and the appropriate treatment. If the school is using a developmental model or curriculum to choose objectives for social or emotional adjustment, the team should look to that model for future objectives, relying on members, such as the school psychologist, having expertise in emotional and behavioral domains. In any event, the team will want to write new goals and objectives for the upcoming year that build on last year's mastery. Goals might address teaching new "replacement behavior" skills or else further increasing or generalizing those newly developed skills, with the goal of having those skills exhibited with greater frequency and reliability than they are now or exhibited in different settings than they are now. Teacher input will clarify whether the child needs new objectives or further consolidation of existing objectives.

6. LRE

Problems that occur in the emotional and behavioral domains often trigger placement change to a more restrictive setting, to an equal or greater extent than problems in other domains. For that reason, it is essential to determine, based in part on teacher and administrator input, whether the child's present performance on target behaviors in those domains is roughly in conformance with expectations for mainstreamed children. If the child presently is served in a special education setting because of behaviors and has made progress on behavioral objectives so that present performance might support success in the mainstream, the team must consider increasing the child's time spent in the mainstream. Similarly, the IEP team must address LRE for the mainstreamed child with behavior problems receiving behavior management as a supplementary aid or service, possibly along with related services, to address those problems. If the child is holding his own or showing progress, the mainstream usually will remain appropriate, depending on the type of behavior and the child's anticipated campus and grade placement for the upcoming year. If the child is not making progress or regressing on the behaviors of concern, the team will need to consider whether revision of the behavior management plan, addition of other services, or possibly a change in the objectives, necessitates a change to a more restrictive setting. While teachers ordinarily have the most authoritative opinions regarding what is feasible in their classrooms to control behavior, often the psychologist or behavior specialist will have promising suggestions to promote inclusion.

7. Identifying Evaluation Procedures

Once objectives are selected in the emotional and behavioral domains, as in any other domain, the team must indicate in the IEP, at least in general terms, the type and frequency of evaluation methods to determine progress. Specific evaluation methods should be reflected somewhere in the school's records, and teachers should retain sufficient documentation of the child's progress. While progress on academic skills can be tracked with naturally occurring data sources such as test responses, work sheets, and completed assignments, behavioral progress regardless of the setting will require special documentation and the extra time and effort that requires. Teachers, with the help of team members having specialized expertise in the emotional and behavioral domain, will need to decide what data collection methods are both feasible to implement and adequate to evaluate the child's progress.

V. KEY DELIBERATIONS TO DOCUMENT

Any point that is worth serious discussion by the IEP team deserves mention in the written minutes of the team's deliberations. This is particularly true if the point is disputed, or may be the subject of an appeal. If the team's decisions are questioned in a due process hearing, the written record can help to establish what the team discussed in the meeting even if the members later become unavailable or cannot remember what took place. Of particular importance, the team will want to ensure an unambiguous record of several essential points. (1) Document what current assessment has to say about the nature of the child's emotional and/or behavioral disability, the behaviors or deficits caused by that disability, and the recommended treatment strategies. Document whether team members agree or disagree about the assessment, and the specific assessment findings, if any, that are disputed. Indicate whether further assessment is necessary because the last assessment is no longer accurate. (3) State the child's present performance in emotional and/or behavioral domains. If information about specific behavioral skills and inappropriate behaviors is not described in the IEP or minutes of deliberations, state where this information may be found in the educational record. State what evaluative data the IEP team used to establish present performance and assess progress on past objectives. (4) Describe how the child's present performance in emotional and behavioral domains compares with what is described in the last IEP, and indicate whether the child is making progress in the affected domain. If the child is not making progress, summarize what the team believes to be the problem. Indicate if further assessment is necessary to identify the problem and what questions the assessment is to answer. (5) The team needs to draft and include in the written IEP goals and measurable objectives in emotional and/or behavioral domains for the next year or other period covered by the IEP. (6) Describe, either in general or specific terms, what evaluation of current objectives will be done and when.

VI. INVOKING STOP-GAP MEASURES

As with any other type of IEP team dispute, the team may recess the IEP meeting to address emotional and behavior problems at any point the team feels further assessment is needed, or additional documentation or references need to be reviewed, or outside persons need to be consulted or perhaps invited to join the team, or merely because tensions need time to wind down. Often, a recess, possibly coupled with informal alternative dispute resolution, allows the team members who are in disagreement to find alternatives that will resolve the impasse and produce an acceptable solution, as well as an appropriate IEP for the child.

Chapter 6

THE IEP MEETING TO CHOOSE
RELATED SERVICES

I. BACKGROUND

IEP teams must, of course, consider related services that are necessary to support special education. Related services are those services traditionally considered "non educational" in nature but related to the educational mission. IEP meetings to consider related services sometimes involve disputes and disagreements that require special knowledge and handling to resolve.

Federal law defines "related services" to mean transportation, as well as developmental, corrective, and other supportive services that may be required to assist a handicapped child to benefit from special education. Services specifically mentioned in federal law include: speech pathology and audiology, psychological services, physical and occupational therapy, orientation and mobility services, recreation, and medical and counseling services. Medical services, however, can be for diagnostic and evaluation purposes only. Related services further include early identification and assessment of handicapping conditions in children.

This list of related services in the federal law is not an exclusive list, and states may provide for additional related services. States also may consider some of the above services as "education" rather than "related services," particularly if the service involves giving the child some type of instruction. Clearly, some related services such as speech therapy are instructional by their nature and relate directly to objectives of the educational curriculum. It will be helpful in reading this chapter to distinguish related services that do not involve any kind of instruction, such as transportation or school health services, from related services that do provide instruction, such as speech therapy, occupational therapy, or social skill training.

Standard for Related Services

IEP meetings to consider related services often get into a discussion of what related services might be helpful or beneficial for the child. However, IEP team members should keep in mind the federal standard for related services. IDEA does not create a "maximizing benefit" standard for related services. If it did, all public schools likely would be obligated to provide any related service that is found to be helpful. Rather, under the federal standard, related services must have some demonstrable necessity, so that without the related service the child's special education could not be effective.

You should understand that states are free to adopt a higher standard than the federal law, and some states have chosen to do so. If your state is among them, the related service inquiry may be different for you. States that require schools to "maximize" educational benefit to the child with a disability may provide all the services needed, including related services, to allow the child to reach his or her full potential. If that is your situation, you should still follow the procedures recommended here, but substitute in the appropriate test for deciding the child's need for related services that applies in your state, as interpreted for you by your school district's special education counsel. Since "maximizing benefit" states are in the minority, the remaining discussion here will reference the federal standard.

To demonstrate the necessity of a related service, the IEP team must study the child's present performance and progress and must look to assessment by one or more persons with expertise in the related service and to the child's educational need. Under the federal standard, if a particular related service is not required in order to enable the child to benefit from special education, then the IEP team may decide to omit that service. Alternatively, the IEP team may consider providing the service as an enhancement to the child's program.

The IEP team's deliberations regarding related services should focus on three particular concerns: making proper use of current assessment, selecting appropriate IEP goals and objectives for the child's unique educational needs, and determining the necessity of the related service to address those goals and objectives, or otherwise to address educational needs.

Using Current Assessment

As with all IEP issues, the core concern for choosing a related service is whether current assessment supports providing the service. Comprehensive assessment reports often suggest a related service or recommend that further assessment be done to determine the need for a related service. Parents frequently bring the team assessment reports from outside professionals recommending a related service. The problem with using assessment reports alone, however, is that although they typically address the child's disability, they rarely address day-to-day educational needs or establish why the related service is *necessary* to insure the efficacy of some current special education goal or other special education service.

It is possible to obtain assessment addressing the specific question of whether a related service is necessary for this child, at this time, to deal with a specific educational need. An assessment for this purpose usually is done by someone with expertise in the related service and familiar with the child's educational program. Findings of such an assessment should allow the IEP team to resolve the related service issue. Many times, however, current assessment will not address the related service question exactly. For example, the team may be using an existing comprehensive assessment done months ago, or on an outside assessment by a provider who is unfamiliar with the specifics of the child's present performance in school. To deal with such assessment, the team must study the inferences that can be drawn from assessment conclusions and recommendations, as they *would* apply to the child's current IEP, and see if this resolves the issue.

Sometimes, the team will feel confident making such inferences from the assessment report because the assessment findings are still plainly relevant to the child's present performance. This might be true when the assessment establishes that, without the related service, the child cannot perform tasks necessary to function successfully in the classroom, or perform other developmentally appropriate activities, for example, due to a sensory, communication, or physical disability.

If, however, the team is unable to make confident inferences from assessment to establish the necessity of the related service, then the assessment professional and/or related service professional needs to have input to the IEP team on this issue and possibly conduct further assessment. This would be true where it is not clear to the team whether the child would derive any significant benefit from the related service or whether the related service is the only effective way to support other components of the IEP.

If the related service professional's input is needed to determine the necessity of the related service and that person cannot attend the IEP meeting, then the related service professional should be informed in advance of the child's proposed goals and objectives so that he or she can make a report to the committee before the meeting. If, during the course of the IEP meeting, new goals and objectives are proposed that raise a question about the necessity of the related service and the team decides that it requires additional professional input to make a good decision, the IEP meeting should recess to obtain that input as quickly as possible.

Selecting Appropriate IEP Goals, Objectives, and Evaluation

The first and overriding concern is the selection of appropriate educational goals, objectives, and services for the child to include in the IEP. The choice of educational goals, objectives, and services will usually "drive" the deliberations regarding the need for related services. The IEP team's task will be to use current assessment data of the child's strengths and the areas affected by the disability, present performance data, and the child's progression in the appropriate curriculum, to select goals and objectives and schedule special education.

Providers of related services are not, however, necessarily isolated from this essentially educational task of choosing goals, objectives, and special education services. There invariably will be situations where the input of the related service professional may be essential to the selection of appropriate goals, objectives, and strategies for a particular child. The speech therapist with expertise in language development of the deaf child, or the psychologist familiar with psychosocial development of the severely emotionally disturbed child, are but two examples.

Along these same lines, there will be times when the "related service," although technically non-educational, is in effect an integral part of the child's education and cannot easily be separated as merely a supportive service. Speech services, for example, often have a central role in relation to the educational mission. Here, also, the related service professional will be an integral member of the IEP team.

Determining the Necessity of the Related Service

There are three typical kinds of situations where the IEP team will need to consider related service. One situation is where the child's comprehensive assessment and present performance indicates that a service is necessary in order for the child to receive a FAPE in some domain affected by the disability. The service may be a non-educational adjunct, or it may be so integral to the child's school progress, or so intertwined with the educational curriculum's objectives, as to be a part of the educational mission. Speech and language services, interpreter services, low-vision services, orientation and mobility services, or physical/occupational therapy services sometimes implicate such critical domains of a child's school functioning that no educational service could truly be effective without them. This is the easiest related service situation for the IEP team to address. Here, the team, if convinced of the essential nature of the service, must provide it.

Another situation, more problematic in nature, occurs when the related service clearly would be relevant to address a need identified in the child's present performance and affected by the disability, but the service is not critical or essential to the furtherance of the educational mission for the child, nor is the related service tantamount to an educational service. The question here is whether one or more special education components of the IEP either a special education objective or a special education service - would be impossible to implement effectively without the service such that the child would not receive FAPE. Stated another way, would the child receive meaningful educational benefit from instruction on a special education IEP objective, or from a special education service, if the related service were omitted? The IEP team's task here is to decide whether the related service is required or merely an enhancement to an IEP that already delivers FAPE. Depending on the individual child's disability and need, such "gray area" services might include counseling, psychotherapy, occupational therapy, recreation, or music therapy. However, most any service theoretically could fall into this category, in a particular case.

In my experience, it is rare in this second type of situation that the evidence before the IEP team establishes convincingly the necessity of the related service. To demonstrate necessity practically requires a single-subject research study in which the child's IEP is implemented under identical conditions with the related service, then without the service.

Comparing progress across these trials would tend to show whether the child could make meaningful progress on the IEP without the service. But circumstances typically do not present this type of data with adequate controls in place to generate much confidence. Instead, some expert or specialist recommends a related service, and the IEP team chooses to provide that service rather than risk exposing the child to failure. This "insurance policy" approach to related services at least helps to minimize the chance of a bad experience or wasted time for the child, however, it obscures the evaluation of both the related service's true effectiveness and the long-run effects of other IEP components.

The third type of problem situation for related services involves requests or recommendations for health-related services, particularly for medically fragile children. Services such as in-school dispensing of medication, catheterization, positioning, and even maintenance of gastric feeding tubes have been found to be consistent with the school's obligation to the child with a medical disability. Other requests and recommendations, however, are not so easy to resolve. Consider, for example, requests for extensive neurological testing and BEAM studies for the TBI child; extensive skilled nursing care for suctioning and maintenance of the child on a ventilator; twice-weekly psychiatric therapy; and nursing care during transportation to and from school. The need for such services must be occasioned by the existence of an IDEA disability, and the services must be necessary in order for the child to benefit from special education. Usually the medically fragile child's status will readily satisfy these criteria. The problem arises when the services are very expensive or require constant staff attention and/or specialized training.

There is no bright line rule for many quasi-medical related services that are otherwise necessary for the child to participate and succeed in school. Services that require physician training and licensure are not the school's responsibility unless limited to diagnosis and evaluation. As for health services that can be administered by non-physicians, the issues are complex. Schools must consider uncertainties such as whether the service can be provided by someone with the training level of a school nurse or other non-medical school professional and how costly or burdensome it will be for school staff to provide the service. If the IEP team can find no clear precedent to guide the deliberations regarding a particular request or recommendation for an unusual type of health-related service, it is usually wise for all parties to seek competent legal advice regarding the specific request or recommendation.

Over the years I have fielded many questions about the need for transportation, or a particular type of transportation, as well as questions pertaining to both common and obscure health-related services. It would take something of a scholarly text to address the technicalities of IEP team decisions about such non-instructional related services. The more typical and, in my opinion, interesting questions, however, concern related services that are essentially instructional in nature or closely integrated with instruction. Consequently, the following material in this chapter is geared mainly to IEP team decisions regarding those types of services.

II. WHAT DOCUMENTATION SHOULD THE TEAM HAVE AVAILABLE TO CONSIDER, AND WHY?

1. The Most Recent Comprehensive Individual Assessment

The current comprehensive assessment and any other current assessment should tell the IEP team the nature of the child's identified disability and the areas of academic deficiency caused by, or related to, that disability. When supplemented by the statement of present performance, current assessment also identifies specific domains and skills affected by the disability. The need for a related service must be occasioned by the existence of a disability and must be linked by necessity to a disability-related special education objective or service. The team thus should use current assessment to specify the nature of the disability, identify domains skills currently affected by the disability, write objectives to address those skills, and provide related services as needed for the child to benefit.

2. The Most Recent IEP Documents

For a child already receiving special education services, the IEP team should compare the child's statement of present performance with the last IEP's objectives and performance levels to see what progress the child made since the last IEP was written. If the child received a related service for which goals and objectives are appropriate, the team should also study the nature of those objectives, the child's progress, and how the objectives fit in to the educational program. The team is then in a position to assess, at least in a general sense, the effectiveness of the last "package" of strategies, including the related service. If the child has received a related service and made progress, this speaks for continuing the same general approach including providing the related service. If the child has not received a related service and made progress without it, the team has some evidence that service may not be necessary, so long as the future IEP objectives and strategies follow a logical progression. If, however, the child has not been making progress in one or more domains affected by the disability, this fact may give some additional support to adding the related service if the proposed objectives and strategies of the related service are in the affected domain and incident to special education objectives where progress has been slow.

3. Parent Records

As with any IEP issue, the team should consider any information the parent brings that is relevant to the child's need for a particular related service. Related service issues often stir strong feelings among parents and other IEP team members, and this is all the more reason to make careful, well-reasoned deliberations. For example, parents frequently bring assessment reports of outside professionals recommending some service for the school to provide and feel appropriately justified in demanding the service. Outside expert reports, however well-meaning and professionally qualified, usually do not have a good understanding of the school's mission, IDEA's mandates, and the role of non-educational services. The team must carefully deliberate and discuss the issues raised by such reports and obtain further assessment or input as needed from professionals in the domain of the related service.

4. Teacher Records

Information from the child's classroom teacher will be important to establish whether the child is making progress and receiving benefit from the related service, or at least from the "package" of IEP services including the related service. Obviously, the child's special education teacher, who is responsible for implementing and/or evaluating goals and objectives for instruction, can help the team explore the relationship between the related service and special education. At the same time, if the child receives supplementary aids and services to support mainstreaming, the regular education teacher's input also will be important if the related service is tied to one or more of those supplementary aids or services or to the mainstreaming itself. The classroom teacher can help the team assess the impact of the related service on the child's classroom functioning.

5. Administrative Records

Administrative records may be helpful with respect to related services that support IEP objectives addressing inappropriate behaviors. For example, disciplinary referrals, removals from the classroom, or "crisis intervention" incidents are often the focus of IEP goals and objectives or the evaluation thereof. By providing the basis for evaluating the program as a whole, this data can also help evaluate the need for and the effectiveness of a related service such as counseling or behavior management consultation.

6. School Health Records

While this chapter does not address the decision-making process for unusual health related service requests, keep in mind that school health records should be studied carefully in such cases for the information they provide relative to the child's present performance and the need for the related service.

7. Related Service Records

If the child is receiving a related service that involves some type of instruction or other direct work with the child, or has an evaluation by a provider of a related service, the logs, reports and recommendations of the provider will bear directly on the IEP team's deliberations. Those records will reflect the IEP objectives of the related service, or else the educational objectives which the related service supports, and may help to document evaluation of the child's progress on those objectives along with the strategies that have been helpful or not helpful. This information is of obvious importance for selecting appropriate future IEP objectives and strategies. Even related services that do not involve instruction generate logs and other kinds of records that may become important in assessing whether the child receives FAPE, such as whether medications were administered, transportation delivered, crisis intervention needed, or interpreter services provided as scheduled.

III. WHO SHOULD BE PRESENT AT THE IEP TEAM MEETING TO CHOOSE RELATED SERVICES AND WHY?

1. The Parent

As with all IEP meetings, the parent should be present to speak for the child's interests. During deliberations concerning related services that involve a specialized service or instruction, the parent along with other team members may take a back seat to persons with specialized training and experience regarding that service, such as speech therapists, physical or occupational therapists, psychologists, nurses, and persons providing medical assessment. The IEP team would be ill-advised to rely heavily on opinions of any individual team members who are not experts, when making decisions that require specialized expertise.

2. The Child's Special Education Teacher

Usually the special education teacher is responsible for instructing the child on special education objectives or at least monitoring the child's progress. The special education teacher also is usually the person to monitor supplementary aids and services provided by special education in the mainstream setting. Thus, the special education teacher can usually pinpoint specific IEP skills and deficits that might be addressed through related services and assist the team in determining whether the related service is necessary to address those concerns. The special education teacher's opinions will be valuable in deliberating the need for related services that involve direct instruction or training with the child. The special education teacher should be familiar with the training and skills of educators working with the child, and the educational strategies within the competency of educators, and can bring this knowledge to bear on the question whether some educational strategy might be as effective as a proposed related service to address the area of concern.

3. The Child's Regular Education Teacher

If the child receives or may receive regular education services, the regular education teacher is a necessary participant in IEP deliberations. This teacher's input will be important in discussing related services that address IEP objectives taught in the regular education setting. When the regular education teacher is directly involved with that service, the teacher also will have valuable input. For example, interpreter services, or speech and occupational therapy delivered in the regular classroom, will directly affect the regular teacher's work and the child's performance in that setting. For many non-instructional types of related services such as transportation, the regular education teacher may have minimal involvement or input.

4. A School Administrator

An administrator or designee must attend the IEP meeting as an official representative of the school district, authorized to commit the district's resources necessary for implementing the IEP. Often, the administrator also will have information relative to behavioral and social adjustment of the student that may be important to consider in developing goals and objectives for related services. The administrator as instructional leader may be the appropriate person to chair the IEP team.

5. Related Service Providers

It is, of course, essential for related service providers to have input at an IEP meeting to consider related services. Often, however, schools do not require related service providers to attend IEP meetings in order to maximize their time available for delivering services to children. So, the related service provider typically drafts proposed goals, objectives, and a schedule of services, in a tentative related-service IEP, and submits it to the IEP team. The team considers the proposed IEP and either adopts it or schedules further assessment to help resolve doubts about it. If team members anticipate, before meeting, difficulty deciding appropriate related services, the team can arrange in advance for the related service provider to attend. If an unanticipated dispute arises during the team meeting, the team can recess the meeting in order to arrange for the provider's presence. If the parent wants more information about related service goals, objectives, or strategies, the related service provider should schedule a mutually convenient time to communicate with the parent individually. When a dispute arises over related services, the IEP team should compare and weigh the different opinions offered concerning the related service, against the background, experience, and qualifications of the person voicing the opinion, and the extent to which the opinion is relevant to educational manifestations and needs created by the disability.

6. Assessment Specialists

A person must be present at the IEP team meeting who can interpret assessment results that are relevant to the team's deliberations. If the related service provider needs to discuss assessment results, he or she should plan to attend the meeting or else find another assessment specialist to attend who can understand the related service assessment and interpret it to the parent and the other IEP team members.

IV. THE ORDER OF BUSINESS FOR IEP TEAM MEMBERS

1. The Chairperson

The person who conducts the IEP team meeting where related services are being discussed should have a working knowledge of how to choose appropriate goals and objectives and how non-educational-related services are supposed to fit into the IEP puzzle. Usually, this person will be a special education appraisal specialist or supervisor. This person needs to orchestrate the meeting to insure input from appraisal specialists, regular and special education teachers, and related service providers. This person also must be able to state assessment findings and teacher evaluation results in a manner comprehensible to parents who are not trained in education-related fields, and create an atmosphere in which parent input is valued and carefully considered by other members of the team.

2. The Opening

The chair of the IEP meeting should begin by summarizing the purpose of the meeting, including a statement that the team will discuss related services. Clarify that the discussion of related services will address the need for the related service, if any, the objectives to be addressed, and the amount of time and schedule for the related service, if appropriate. The chair should inquire if the parent is satisfied with the notice of the meeting, understands the reason for the meeting and the order of business, and has any request to alter or add to the agenda. The chair should review the order of discussions for the meeting.

3. Presenting Assessment Information and Identifying Present Performance

The IEP team must examine the current assessment to make sure members have an understanding of the academic and non-academic domains affected by the child's disability. Then the team should hear from teachers and specialists working with the child to review evaluative data and update the statement of present performance. The team should also examine present performance from the perspective of the parent, particularly in domains affected by related services. The selection of goals, objectives, and strategies, including related services, is guided by the conclusions and recommendations of current assessment and the statement of present performance.

4. Choosing Goals and Objectives

After studying the current assessment, the team will want to write appropriate IEP goals and objectives for the next year that build on last year's mastery or if the child ismainstreamed, continue the child at the next level in the regular curriculum with supplementary aids and services. At this point, the team can review goals and objectives to determine which require the provision of related services in order for the child to succeed.

5. Choosing and Scheduling Related Services

At this stage the team should review the IEP objectives that may require additional support of related services and consider the recommendations of related service professionals and other members of the IEP team. The team must decide which services are necessary, the amount and timing of each service, and how and where the service should be delivered. If the service is not instructional in nature, the team should record these deliberations and schedule the related service.

6. Identifying Evaluation Procedures

If a related service scheduled by the IEP team is instructional in nature, the team should further discuss how that related service is to be evaluated. Normally, the related service provider, if not present at the IEP meeting, will have written a report for the team indicating the evaluation schedule and methods. If this information has been omitted from the report and the provider is not present at the meeting, the team still may be able to schedule evaluation when the related service objective is the same as an instructional IEP objective. The evaluation methods chosen for the educational objective could serve as the evaluation of the supporting related service as well, if the team thinks that appropriate. If, however, the team feels that more specialized evaluation is needed for the related service, the team should recess and obtain the input of the related service provider regarding evaluation. The team may then reconvene and include or reference in the IEP the evaluation for the related service.

V. KEY DELIBERATIONS TO DOCUMENT

Any point that is worth serious discussion by the IEP team deserves mention in the written minutes of the team's deliberations. This is particularly true if the point is disputed or may be the subject of an appeal. If the team's decisions are questioned in a due process hearing, the written record can help to establish what the team discussed in the meeting even if the members later become unavailable or cannot remember what took place. Of particular importance, the team will want to ensure an unambiguous record of several points. (1) Documentation should make clear which assessment the team relied on to identify the nature and effects of the disability justifying the selection of related services. This is particularly important when the team decides not to provide a service that someone has proposed, or discontinues a related service that has previously been provided, because the disability does not affect the educational domain of that service. One example is where a counselor feels that the child would benefit from weekly individual counseling to enhance functioning, but the assessment shows that the child's disability does not affect emotional, behavioral, or social functioning. Or where someone proposes special transportation as a related service, but the child's disability does not affect his or her ability to use standard transportation modes. If there is disagreement on the team about the assessment, the record should indicate areas of disagreement and whether further assessment is necessary.

(2) Documentation should clearly state the child's present performance in areas affected by the disability or indicate where such information can be found in the child's records. The statement of present

performance is the foundation for writing goals and objectives and thus for choosing related services of an instructional nature to support them. If the team decides to discontinue a related service, the statement of present performance should establish that the child's skills in the affected domain have progressed to the point of not requiring related service support.

(3) The record should make clear the basis for the team's decision that a particular related service is, or is not, "necessary" for the child to benefit from special education. Deliberations about the necessity of related services often pit one team member against another and evoke strong opinions and feelings. Team members should muster their data from assessments, progress evaluations, and current levels of performance in order to show that a particular decision about related services is "reasonably calculated" to benefit the child. Examining this data carefully, and making only those inferences that logically can be drawn from it, exemplifies proper use of IDEA's procedural safeguards.

VI. INVOKING STOP-GAP MEASURES

If despite the foregoing the team finds itself in disagreement over the provision of related services, the team may recess the IEP meeting, as mentioned in the preceding discussion of IDEA procedural options, at any point the team feels further assessment is needed, or additional documentation needs to be reviewed, or outside persons need to be consulted or made part of the team, or merely because tensions need time to wind down. Often, a recess, possibly coupled with informal alternative dispute resolution, allows the team members who are in disagreement to find alternatives that will resolve the impasse and produce an acceptable solution. Proper use of IDEA's procedural safeguards is the best insurance policy for obtaining an appropriate IEP.

Chapter 7

THE IEP MEETING TO ADDRESS METHODOLOGY

I. BACKGROUND

What Is Methodology?

What exactly is meant by "methodology?" There are several things that it is not. It is not a goal or objective. It is not, in and of itself, a special education service, a supplementary aid or service, a placement, or an assistive technology service. It is not specifically defined in the federal special education statutes and regulations. Yet the choice of methodology may be inextricably bound up in the essential deliberations of the IEP team regarding services, placement, technology, and even goals and objectives.

One approach is to view methodology as a manner or technique for implementing a service based on a theory or on research findings that predict a relationship between the manner of intervention and outcomes. Most any educational objective lends itself to a variety of instructional methods to achieve that objective. Word recognition can be taught in different ways, such as with phonics, a sight-word method, a multisensory method, or a combination of these. Deaf students can learn classroom communication skills via ASL, SEE and its variants, cued speech, speech reading, or "total communication." Self-injurious behavior can be addressed through behavior modification involving DRI with fixed or variable schedules, alone or in combination with positive punishment, negative punishment, and even harsh aversives. A child's classroom depression symptoms can be treated by various combinations of methods including medication, counseling, activity therapies, and behavior modification. These different approaches or strategies might be thought of as aspects of methodology.

102

Who Chooses Methodology

Instructional personnel ought to be free to choose methods based on empirical support regarding their effectiveness to address the problem at hand. Commentaries to IDEA reauthorization reinforce this concept that schools have the responsibility and authority to select among appropriate methodologies. In an ideal world, if one method or approach were undisputedly the "best practice," there would be no need to choose, strictly speaking. One simply uses the method that gives the "best" result, with no reason to deliberate or argue. However, IEP teams most often get involved in methodology issues and disputes when there is no convincing research that demonstrates the superiority of one method over another for a discrete, homogeneous group of children with characteristics resembling the child whose IEP in question. Special education incorporates countless methodologies, which is one of its strengths. But these methodologies often lack outcome studies comparing their effectiveness against other methods with discrete groups of children. That is one of special education's vulnerabilities. Indeed, the very notion of providing special education as a separate educational service lacks consistent research support.

There is another problem in approaching methodology choice even when outcome studies are available. One methodology may have empirical support for remediating a specific problem in a large, more or less homogeneous sample of children. Yet, the success of that methodology with a large group of children in a research or standardization sample does not necessarily predict success with any individual child. The likelihood of a methodology's success with a child decreases as differences increase between the characteristics of the child in question and the characteristics of the research group. Often, the only approach to finding out whether a particular method works with a child is to implement that method with the child in a "single-subject" trial, collecting and analyzing outcome data to see if the method produces meaningful benefit.

Because outcome research is often lacking for a particular method or, when available, does not support confident outcome predictions about a specific child, the methodology preference of a parent or school district often comes down to issues not directly related to FAPE, such as economic cost, publisher's unsupported claims, or the bare testimonials of parents or teachers concerning other children. These issues make fertile ground for disagreement and litigation.

Perhaps, in recognition of the large array of available methods, the staggering complexity of educational disabilities, and the ambiguity of research findings, courts have tended to give school officials discretion in choosing methodology, so long as the school's chosen methodology delivers FAPE. Drafters of IDEA reauthorization reinforce this principle. To deliver FAPE (in most states), the child's individualized program must be reasonably calculated to enable the child to receive meaningful educational benefit, that is, to make progress in the general education curriculum or on special education IEP objectives that are appropriate and challenging. Thus, to the extent methodology is implicated in FAPE delivery, the IEP team ordinarily is not required to choose the best method but only the method that will result in meaningful gains. Deliberations over methodology often do not directly affect other IEP issues such as placement, LRE, or choice of related services and technology. Disagreements involving methodology alone typically end with the school district getting at least an opportunity to try the method preferred by educators so long as the method is "reasonable," which usually means that it has some relevant empirical support.

When Does Methodology Affect FAPE?

Methodology issues create more complexity in three common types of situations: (1) when the school or the parent contends that the methodology is necessary for FAPE; (2) when the choice of methodology requires, or supports, a particular placement on the LRE continuum; or (3) when the choice of methodology requires controversial interventions that might be considered questionable. When such complications occur, school officials will not necessarily have the discretion to choose methodology. The court or hearing officer may gauge the child's need according to a different legal standard, for example, the standard for LRE, supplementary aids and services, or assistive technology, that affords the school less discretion.

In one hypothetical example, methodology may be interrelated with both assistive technology and LRE. If a child could achieve meaningful benefit in a self-contained placement from either a relatively simple, inexpensive communication device or a much more sophisticated and costly computer-assisted device with a voice synthesizer, the school's choice might prevail. However, if the more sophisticated device would enable the child to function successfully in regular education classes, where the simpler device would not, then the child's need for the device might be judged according to the standard for supplementary aids and services, rather than methodology, and the school's choice might not prevail.

Some methodologies are simply too controversial for courts to allow their use on a discretionary basis. With self-injurious behavior, for example, experts consider a variety of management techniques, ranging from positive reinforcement of incompatible behavior to mild punishment to radical techniques such as punishment with electric shock. Even for behaviors that do not cause self-injury, some educators have resorted to "boot camp" style interventions involving extended work periods, food deprivation, and social punishment. Courts will study the more controversial techniques carefully, particularly those involving the use of punishment to modify behavior, and schools should not expect the deference ordinarily accorded methodology decisions.

Some methodologies by their very nature are so comprehensive that the methodology choice is wrapped up in the issue of FAPE delivery. For example, certain approaches with autistic children, such as the Lovaas method, require so much highly structured time that the method, as a practical matter, is the program itself. Some communication methods with deaf children, in theory, purport to be so integrally involved with the child's acquisition of English language skills that educators or parents have attempted to make the choice of such methods a FAPE issue. And the use of certain methods used widely in the education of seriously emotionally disturbed children such as level systems and point systems or token economies as a practical matter are necessarily involved with the choice of placement in the LRE.

The Foundation: Proper Use of Assessment to Choose Methodology

The child's comprehensive assessment is almost always the starting point for questions concerning provision of FAPE, and the choice of appropriate methodology does not differ from other IEP issues in this regard. The assessment of a child's learning style, given the nature and severity of the disability, is particularly important in helping to guide methodology choices. Assessment should describe the child's learning characteristics, strengths, and disability related deficits. A child with developmental learning disorders, for example, may have particular strengths in verbal skills, visuo-spatial skills, or perceptual-motor skills. If a methodology teaches to areas where the child has particular strength, the approach will tend to accelerate the learning of new material but do nothing to bolster deficit areas. This is not necessarily inappropriate. Assessment can help to determine the pros and cons of "teaching to" the child's strengths versus building up the child's deficit areas. If a particular methodology emphasizes areas where the child has deficits, assessment will help explore to what extent deficit areas are remediable. If disability-related deficit areas are remediable to some extent, assessment can help determine the extent of instructional resources appropriate to direct toward maintaining or improving skills in those areas. If deficit areas are not remediable, assessment can help show ways the child can work around those areas to achieve appropriate goals and objectives.

Advances in technology will continue to affect the assessment of strengths and deficit areas for children with disabilities, along with the selection of appropriate methodology. Improvements in such areas as cochlear implant technology, software-assisted communication, and low-vision enhancement will force educators and IEP teams to continue reconceptualizing methodology issues that were once thought to be fairly well-settled.

Identifying Present Performance

The child's present performance levels may affect methodology choices directly, if the methodology's appropriate implementation requires baseline skills that are not in the child's repertoire because of age, skill level, or the effects of a disability. For example, a deaf child's parents in one case requested immediate implementation of cued-speech instruction to facilitate increased mainstreaming, where the child previously was being instructed exclusively via total communication in a primarily self-contained setting. New assessment revealed that the child could function in the general education setting to a greater extent with cued-speech, after cued-speech skills were built up. The school district was able to justify a gradual transition of the child from the total communication program to the cued-speech program by showing that the child's cued-speech skills, while susceptible of development, would require a period of months to develop to the extent necessary to support increased mainstreaming. Thus, the immediate implementation of cued speech as the sole methodology was not appropriate.

Present performance levels also can affect methodology choices indirectly. When compared with the child's last statement of performance, the present performance data can be used to assess the extent to which the child has made progress with the current methodology. This approximates the single-subject evaluative approach mentioned earlier, where the child's own performance over time establishes whether a particular approach has been effective. The best justification for choosing a particular methodology lies in the present performance data, if those data establish that the child has made meaningful progress on appropriate educational objectives using that methodology. Given the dearth of relevant research data on most methodological approaches, it is very difficult to support change to a different proposed methodology when the child has been successful with the current methodology. The examination of present performance levels is necessary not only to document progress from the past but also to establish baseline for the next evaluative period.

Selection of Goals and Objectives

Ordinarily, the IEP team chooses goals and objectives for the child's IEP, and the school district staff selects the methodology most appropriate for the child to achieve those goals and objectives. The selection of the goals and objectives is the first and primary choice for the IEP team. The selection of methods is secondary and left to the judgment of teachers or other educational service providers. If the IEP goals and objectives are appropriate and challenging for the child, the short-term objectives are stated in measurable behavioral terms, and the school's chosen methods enable the child to make progress, then the IEP team and the school have performed their respective jobs correctly.

However, when methodology becomes entangled with other issues, such as FAPE or LRE, the choice of both objectives and methodology may require an interactive process. For example, a methodology may be so comprehensive that it has its own curriculum, with associated developmental objectives, in one or more domains of instruction. Or, alternatively, the methodology may dictate objectives indirectly, as where a particular communication method or teaching system is involved, and some objectives make more sense than others in light of the unique approach to instruction. In any event, in those occasional situations where the child's disability makes a specific methodology necessary to deliver FAPE or to educate the child in the LRE, the choice of goals and objectives must relate logically to the required methodology.

Evaluation

Selection and appropriate use of evaluation methods in the present IEP will be necessary to document progress and thus help shed light on methodology issues that may arise in the future. Parents and school staff both have an interest in verifying that educational methods selected by the school are appropriate and enable the child to progress on appropriate goals and objectives. The use of standardized tests versus criterion-referenced measured for evaluation purposes has already been discussed, along with potential uses of the single-subject study to compare student progress using different services or different methodologies. It is extremely important for the IEP team facing uncertainty or a possible disagreement regarding methodology to insure that short-term objectives are written in measurable behavioral terms to make them susceptible to evaluation for documenting progress.

If the child is failing to derive benefit from the IEP and/or the instructional approaches chosen by the school, the evaluation data should help to identify domains affected by the disability where progress is lacking. When both objectives and services are judged appropriate in light of the comprehensive assessment and current classroom assessment data, the IEP team may be able to infer that the school's choice of methodology is the culprit and make necessary adjustments.

II. WHAT DOCUMENTATION SHOULD THE TEAM HAVE AVAILABLE TO CONSIDER AND WHY?

1. The Most Recent Comprehensive Individual Assessment

Current comprehensive assessment should inform the IEP team about the nature of the child's disability, and the learning style, strengths, and deficits the child may exhibit that are affected by, or related to, that disability. If the comprehensive assessment leaves the IEP team puzzled about which sorts of strategies might be effective for educating the child and current teacher evaluative data do not clarify this information for the team, then it is time to update the assessment, particularly where team members are not satisfied with the child's progress.

2. The Most Recent IEP Documents

If the child is already receiving special education services, the IEP team should examine the last IEP documents for the statement of present performance and the last set of goals and objectives. The team should compare the child's last statement of present performance against the evaluation data for the IEP's objectives to determine what progress the child made. The teacher should have test data, work sheets, and other records to illustrate progress. If no progress can be established, the IEP team should take appropriate steps, including obtaining further assessment, to determine whether the child's lack of progress is caused by the severity of the disability itself, the choice of inappropriate goals and objectives, the nature and amount of special education and related services, or (finally) the choice of methodology.

3. Parent Records

Even though methodology choice is usually within the discretion of school staff and ordinarily is not an IEP issue, the IEP team nevertheless should consider any information the parent offers that is relevant to the evaluation of student progress and the selection of appropriate methodology. School staff should be prepared to describe how their chosen methodology is similar to or different from the methodology proposed by the parent. If the parent is not satisfied with the school's methodology, school staff should be prepared to justify their choice by showing how the methodology is bringing about progress of the child on appropriate IEP objectives. If methodology becomes an IEP issue, for one of the reasons discussed earlier, the school should be prepared to engage in serious dialogue to consider the appropriateness of different proposed methodologies and choose an approach tailored to the child's individual needs that has a demonstrable track record of success for children with similar characteristics. While the IEP team is not bound to pick the "best" methodology, the approach that is chosen should support meaningful gains on behavioral skills that are developmentally challenging to the child.

4. Teacher Records

Teacher information will be the most important information for the IEP team to consider should a legitimate methodology dispute arise.

Classroom examinations, assignments, work sheets and other records produced by the child in the regular or special education setting can show graphically the child's strengths, deficits, and developmental characteristics directly relevant to the choice of appropriate methodology. Notes and other anecdotal teacher information fill in details profiling the child's needs and learning characteristics. Without this data, available only from classroom teachers, the IEP team may deliberate irrelevant methodology based on information, such as publisher's unsupported advertising claims, that has no applicability to the child in question.

5. Related Service Records

While related services tend to involve specialized technical skills and clinical judgments, IEP teams nevertheless face occasional challenges to related service methodology by persons without specific training in the area of the related service. Because of this, the school's related service staff should be prepared to justify their choice of methods in their field of specialization and to document the child's progress using that chosen method. If the child is not making meaningful gains with the method chosen by the school's related service provider, the IEP team should be prepared to order further assessment relative to the domain addressed by the related service, including an assessment of whether the related service remains appropriate, and why, along with recommendations to improve the delivery of the related service if it remains appropriate.

III. WHO SHOULD BE PRESENT AT THE IEP TEAM MEETING TO CONSIDER METHODOLOGY, AND WHY?

1. The Parent

As with all IEP meetings, the parent should be present as the representative of the child and the person who, under IDEA, has the right to speak for the child's interests.

2. The Child's Special Education Teacher

If the child is already receiving special education services, the special education teacher brings essential evaluative data to the IEP team regarding present performance and progress on IEP goals and objectives. In addition to bringing evaluative data and a description of the child's present performance, the teacher should be able to explain the methods used to address IEP objectives and the rationale for their selection in light of the child's disability and learning characteristics. If the child receives some education in the general education setting and a general education teacher cannot attend the IEP team meeting, the special education teacher should collect and report information from general education teachers.

3. The Child's Regular Education Teacher

If the child receives or may receive instruction in a general education setting, it is preferable that the child's teacher or teachers from that setting attend the IEP team meeting to describe the child's progress. If an issue arises regarding some specialized method for delivering a supplementary aid or service, such as an assistive device, modification, or communication method, the general education teacher is in the position to evaluate the impact of that aid or service on the child's progress. If the general education teacher cannot attend the IEP team meeting, he or she should provide an oral or written summary of the relevant information to the special education teacher to present during the IEP team's deliberations.

4. A School Administrator

An administrator or someone designated by the school administration must attend the meeting as an official school representative with authority to commit the district's resources necessary to implement the IEP. The administrator, as campus instructional leader, may be the appropriate person to chair the IEP team, deferring as necessary to other team members with expertise regarding any methodology that is the subject of discussion or disagreement.

5. Other Assessment Specialists

Assessment specialists and providers of related services should be present at the IEP team meeting, or otherwise have input to the team, in any areas affected by the disability where specialized data or assessment data is necessary for the deliberations, or where the type or method of related service requires discussion. A person must be present at the IEP team meeting who can interpret assessment results that are relevant to the team's deliberations.

IV. THE ORDER OF BUSINESS FOR IEP TEAM MEMBERS

1. The Chairperson

The person who conducts an IEP team meeting convened specifically to address an issue of methodology should be a person having background in the instructional area affected by the methodology, knowledge regarding the child's disability, and familiarity with assessment and evaluation methods. Often this is a special education appraisal specialist or supervisor. This person needs to orchestrate the meeting to insure input from the parent and from other IEP team members with information relevant to the method or methods in question. The chairperson must be able to report assessment findings and evaluation results in a manner comprehensible to persons without specific training in these areas and to create an atmosphere in which the entire group can function as a team.

2. The Opening

Following introductions, the chair of the IEP meeting should begin by summarizing the purpose of the meeting, indicating that the team will review assessment, goals and objectives, present performance, and the specific methodology issue raised by the parent or school staff. The chair should present the proposed order of presentations, including the parent and/or their representatives, as well as the school district's representatives. The chair should inquire if the parent is satisfied with the notice received concerning the timing and content of the meeting, understands the order of business, and has any request to alter the agenda, raise additional issues for consideration, or present additional matter to the team.

3. Presenting Assessment Information and Identifying Present Performance

The IEP team must examine current assessment, with special attention areas of the child's functioning affected by the disability, and the child's learning characteristics including strengths and deficit areas. If assessment data do not create a helpful picture of the child's characteristics, or if observed characteristics are not congruent with information contained in the assessment, the team should consider ordering further assessment and deferring further deliberations until current satisfactory assessment is available. The team should have an understanding of the child's developmental and learning characteristics before discussing issues of methodology.

4. Identifying Present Performance

If the assessment appears current, the team should go on to elicit information from the child's teacher about the child's present performance in areas affected by the disability. It is essential to review the evaluation of objectives scheduled in the previous annual IEP meeting. If the child is mainstreamed and receives aids and services to address effects of the disability, the IEP team must have input from the teacher to determine if the child is mastering regular curriculum objectives and passing tests with the help of the aids and services.

If the Child Is Making Progress in the LRE

If the child has made meaningful progress mastering special education objectives in the areas affected by the disability, or mastering general education curriculum objectives where appropriate, and the team is satisfied that the child is being educated in the LRE, then the IEP team has no need to engage in a discussion of methodology at all, at least in theory. This is because of the school's discretion regarding methodology choice, and the federal definition of FAPE. However, it is also true that a parent must be afforded the right to present information to the IEP team, and may wish to discuss a methodology issue despite the child's making adequate progress. And even though federal law and most states do not require schools to "maximize" the progress of students with disabilities, most parents and school staff in truth want to see each child get the best education possible, within the limits of the child's disability and the school's resources. Parents are looking for every opportunity to improve their child's progress, and most teachers read books and attend workshops whenever they can to learn better ways of working with disabled children. For these reasons, most IEP team members are more than willing to discuss and should discuss promising methodology developments. Hopefully it is in this spirit that IEP teams address concerns and debates about methodology, constrained only by the realities of limited school resources to serve all disabled and non-disabled children.

If the Child Is Not Making Progress

If, however, the review of present performance indicates the child is not making meaningful progress on scheduled objectives, the team needs to examine all assessment data and the IEP carefully to determine what caused the child's failure. A thorough, competent and up-to-date assessment may reveal that the child's disability is just too severe to expect meaningful progress in the domains targeted by IEP goals and objectives. If that is the case, the team should rethink the goals and objectives. The evaluation, present performance, and teacher data may reveal that the child is learning but for some reason is not able to complete assignments, take tests, or progress at the expected rate. Any of these shortcomings should trigger discussion of ways of improving IEP services, including special education, related services, or aids and services in the mainstream, to provide more assistance or better assistance to the child. If it appears, however, that the child's failure is not caused by the selection of inappropriate objectives or by the type or amount of special education services, the IEP team will inevitably have to address the issue of methodology and examine approaches and strategies more carefully.

5. Choosing Appropriate Methodology

Once the IEP team has decided to try a different methodology, either because the child is failing or because the team wants to encourage more progress, the task is to choose the methodology most likely to enable the child to succeed on appropriate goals and objectives in the LRE. How should the team go about this? Since relatively few methodology cases have made it into the law books and few states have adopted a "maximizing benefit" standard, the law offers little guidance in choosing methodology, so long as the chosen methodology delivers FAPE in the LRE! So educators must instead look to their own professional literature to address this issue. The IEP team should locate a resource person, for example a master teacher, private consultant, or university professor, with knowledge relevant to the child's disabling condition, as well as expertise in the technology of instruction in the domain or domains where the child is failing. This person should be familiarized with the individual child's assessed learning characteristics, strengths, and deficit areas. With this information, the resource person should be in a position to identify alternative methodologies for the IEP team to consider, along with the rationale, pros, and cons of each. Ideally, one or more methodologies will be backed up by independent research support demonstrating its effectiveness with children having characteristics similar to the child whose IEP is in question. The team then is in a position to choose a methodology to attempt with the child.

6. Identifying Evaluation Procedures

Once the IEP team has chosen the methodology and identified appropriate goals and objectives, the team must design, and reference in the IEP, evaluation methods to determine progress. If the IEP team ever reaches the point of having to address methodology because of a child's school failure, having ruled out all of the other IEP issues that might be at fault, chances are the child's unique situation is particularly difficult. For this reason, designing and adhering to appropriate evaluation methods will be critical to identify what works for the child. School staff and parents should design, use, and retain sufficient documentation of the child's work, such as test responses, work sheets, or completed assignments, to show whether the child is progressing. A special education teacher must maintain regular contact with the child's general education teacher to insure adequate documentation of the child's progress in mainstream classes.

V. KEY DELIBERATIONS TO DOCUMENT

Any point that is worth serious discussion by the IEP team deserves mention in the written minutes of the team's deliberations. This is particularly true if the point is disputed or may be the subject of an appeal. If the team's decisions are questioned in a due process hearing, the written record can help to establish what the team discussed in the meeting even if the members later become unavailable or cannot remember what took place.

The IEP team that considers methodology issues will want to record several important points. (1) Document what current assessment shows to be the child's disability, the domains affected by the disability, and the severity of the disability in each domain. Document what the child's comprehensive assessment and current teacher assessment data establish regarding the child's learning characteristics, strengths, and deficits. State whether team members agree or disagree about the assessment and if there is disagreement, which specific assessment findings are disputed. Indicate whether further assessment is necessary because the last assessment is disputed or is no longer accurate. (2) State the child's present performance in areas affected by the disability. If information about specific skills is not detailed in the IEP itself, indicate where this information is recorded. State what evaluative data the IEP team used to establish performance on past objectives and identify present performance. (3) Describe how present performance data compares with the last IEP and indicate whether the child is, or is not, making progress on IEP objectives or in general education. (4) If the child is making progress, note any objections to the successful methodology. If the team desires to use different methodology to increase performance, the notes should reflect that the child has been receiving appropriate education and that the team agrees the new methodology is being tried solely to enhance the child's program. (5) If the child is not making progress, identify and rule out alternative causes of the child's failure. If it appears that methodology is not effective, state why the team believes this to be so. Indicate if further assessment is necessary, in what areas, and what questions the assessment is to answer. (6) Document procedures that the team used in order to identify alternative methodologies to replace the methodology that the team believes is not being successful. Document the reasons for selecting the methodology that is ultimately chosen, relative to objective research findings and the basis for expecting success of the methodology with the individual child whose IEP is in question. (7) Detail what evaluation of current objectives will be done, when, how, and by whom.

VI. INVOKING STOP GAP MEASURES

As with any other type of IEP meeting, the team may recess the meeting in case of a dispute, as mentioned in the discussion of IDEA procedural options, at any point the team feels further assessment is needed, or additional documentation or references need to be reviewed, or outside persons need to be consulted or perhaps invited to be part of the team, or merely because tensions need time to wind down. Often, a recess, possibly coupled with informal alternative dispute resolution, allows the team members who are in disagreement to find alternatives that will resolve the impasse and produce an acceptable solution, as well as an appropriate IEP for the student.

Chapter 8

THE IEP MEETING TO ADDRESS MEDICAL SERVICES

I. BACKGROUND

Existing IDEA regulations address medical and school health services in general terms, and outline the school's obligation to provide these services under the category of related services. These regulations say that related services may include "medical services for diagnostic or evaluation purposes," as well as "school health services" as provided by "a school nurse or other qualified person" 34 CFR 300.13[a]; 300.16[b][11]. Since related-service language in the reauthorized IDEA did not change regarding medical services, these regulations should be consulted for guidance, pending new regulations. In the principal case interpreting IDEA's medical services language, *Irving ISD v. Tatro*, the U.S. Supreme Court explained that IDEA plainly obligates schools to provide medical evaluation that is necessary to identify a child's disability or need for services but not to provide medical services from a licensed physician. The *Tatro* case did not directly involve the issue of IDEA entitlement to health care services that can legally be provided by a non-physician, and the lower courts that have struggled with this issue have not always agreed.

Tatro set out the two-part inquiry for addressing all medical and health care services for students with disabilities under IDEA. First, the decision maker must initially determine whether the health care service under discussion is a supportive service that is required to assist the child to benefit from special education. If not, then the school has no IDEA obligation to provide the service. For example, if the health care service can be provided at some time other than during the school day, the service is not "necessary" to assist the child in benefitting from special education.

If the health care service is a necessary supportive service, the decision maker must then determine if the service is one that legally can be delivered only by a licensed physician. If the service must be delivered by a licensed physician, the school is obligated to provide the service only if it is for diagnostic and evaluation purposes. The school is not obligated to provide physician services that are not for diagnostic and evaluative purposes. If, however, the service can be provided by someone other than a licensed physician, the school may be obligated to provide the service, even if it is costly and burdensome to do so.

Different courts have reached different conclusions regarding the schools' IDEA obligation to provide health care services that go beyond basic school health needs, such as administering medication. Such services can include things like:

> tracheostomy monitoring
> tracheostomy suctioning
> ventilator setting checks
> ambu bag administration
> gastrostomy monitoring
> urinary bladder catheterization
> bowel disimpaction
> positioning
> blood pressure monitoring
> tube feeding

Some courts have relieved schools from the burden to provide highly specialized and costly health care services. Other courts, however, view such services as mandated by IDEA. The differences stem in part from the interpretation of certain language in *Tatro*.

In dicta, the *Tatro* Court opined that IDEA's definition of "medical services" expressed Congress' desire to "spare schools from an obligation to provide a service that might well prove unduly expensive and beyond the range of their competence." But these dicta were not part of the legally binding decision in the case. As the Court's opinion actually applies to the case's facts, *Tatro* stands only for the proposition that non-physician health care services, which can be provided by a trained lay person or allied health professional, cannot necessarily be excluded from the ambit of IDEA-mandated related services.

After *Tatro*, schools resisted providing complex, expensive health care services to children with disabilities, in reliance on the quoted dicta of that opinion. Indeed, a number of IDEA hearing officers and lower courts espoused that view, thus relieving schools of having to provide health services that required, for example, full-time nursing supervision, inordinately expensive medical equipment, or required highly specialized nursing skills outside the range of a general school health practice. OSEP, the federal agency that monitors IDEA compliance, issued an opinion that tended to broaden, rather than limit, the type and extent of "school health services" that schools must make available to students with disabilities. OSEP said that just about anything can be a "school health service" if (1) the service is necessary for the child to benefit from special education, (2) must be administered during school hours, and (3) can be provided by a trained professional other than a licensed physician. This view is consistent with the *Tatro* holding, though not with the dicta quoted earlier. Another recent OSEP opinion reinforces OSEP's view that a school could, at least in theory, be obligated under IDEA to provide one-on-one nursing care services as a related service, depending on the circumstances of the particular case. OSEP declined to endorse any "bright line" rule saying that one-on-one nursing care constitutes a medical service which schools are never obligated to provide.

Today, the appellate court decisions concerning services by non-physician health care providers tend to adopt one of two approaches. The first approach, prevalent in most jurisdictions, rests on the *Tatro* dicta quoted earlier. This approach determines whether non- physician health care services are within the school's IDEA responsibility based on cost and complexity criteria. Basically, under this approach, schools need not provide services that are unduly complex from a technical standpoint, (e.g. requiring highly specialized nursing personnel), or unduly burdensome from an economic standpoint (e.g. requiring constant, full-time, one-on-one nursing care).

The second approach rests on the *Tatro* holding, which draws a "bright line" only between physician and non-physician services. Courts following this second approach tend to view IDEA as requiring schools to provide any and all required health care services, so long as the services can be delivered by a non-physician provider, regardless of the cost or complexity of the service. Obviously, the reader is urged to consult local counsel to determine which rule is likely to apply in the reader's jurisdiction when it becomes necessary to make a difficult decision regarding school health care services.

The Foundation: Proper Use of Assessment

The child's comprehensive assessment is almost always the starting point for questions concerning provision of FAPE, including questions about appropriate health care related services. Remember that the health care service, in order to be deemed necessary as a related service, must be necessary for the child to benefit from special education. Thus, the health care service must be intended to address some area that is affected by the child's disability. This means the service either (1) necessarily relates to an IEP objective or service or (2) is required in order for the student to be present and learning in school. To decide these issues, the IEP team must consult the comprehensive assessment data to determine the nature of the child's IDEA disability and whether the health care service in question involves a domain affected by the disability.

Admittedly, most of the health care services parents and schools have argued over are the kinds of services that are necessary for the child to be present and functioning in the school environment, reasonably free of life-threatening risks. These are intensive services like ventilator monitoring, suctioning, and ambu bag administration. These are also the services that tend to require more or less continuous presence of trained staff for emergency situations that may arise during the administration of the health care procedures or any other time. Intensive services like this will almost always be related to an IDEA disability and almost always be required for the student to work on special education goals and objectives.

Another issue to be answered by specialized assessment is whether the health care service is necessary in the sense that it must be delivered during the school day and cannot be delivered at some other time. The health care professional who assesses the child's medical disability is the best, if not the only, individual with the background and knowledge to answer this question.

Assessment also may be necessary to address questions about proper training and qualifications of personnel to deliver the health care related service. In at least one dispute, the parents and the school disagreed over the credentials of the proposed service provider. The parents wanted a licensed nurse, and the school proposed to deliver the service through a properly trained aide. The cost difference in public funds between the parents' and the school's proposals was significant. The school prevailed in that dispute, but the result obviously depended heavily on the nature and complexity of the procedure and the training level to be required of the health care aide. These are the kids of decisions that the IEP team can resolve by careful investigation regarding the child's needs and consultation from qualified health care providers.

Identifying Present Performance, Goals, and Objectives

Some health care related services with certain children may involve self-care objectives for which it is appropriate to identify present performance and write IEP goals and objectives. Many children can, for example, learn to self catheterize, and to manage many other aspects of their health care. Indeed they must do so, and the school must teach them to do so, if they are going to be more independent. If a health care related service involves an educational component, that component should be reflected in the statement of present performance and in the IEP goals and objectives. The IEP team should follow the outline of deliberations for selecting and writing appropriate goals and objectives.

In contrast, other health care related services may be necessary purely for health, safety, and maintenance purposes. These services will not involve an educational component for the child. If the service does not involve an IEP objective, there should be no need to address present performance.

Evaluation

For the evaluation of health care related services with an instructional component, the associated IEP objectives should be evaluated in the same manner as other types of instructional objectives. Health care related services lacking such a component should be evaluated for effectiveness by the professional who is responsible for providing or monitoring the service according to the standards of that profession.

II. WHAT DOCUMENTATION SHOULD THE TEAM HAVE AVAILABLE TO CONSIDER AND WHY?

1.The Most Recent Comprehensive Individual Assessment

Current comprehensive assessment should inform the IEP team about the nature of the child's disability, as well as the domains affected by the disability. This information is necessary in some cases to decide whether a particular health care service is necessary as a related service. If the child is eligible for special education because of a medical disability, for example, other health impairment, traumatic brain injury, then the health care related service may be necessary for health maintenance reasons. If so, the IEP team should have documentation of medical, nursing, and other appropriate health care assessment establishing the necessity of the service and the manner of its delivery.

2. The Most Recent IEP Documents

If the child is eligible for special education services and has health care related instructional objectives in the IEP, the IEP team should examine the last IEP documents for the statement of present performance, as well as the last set of goals and objectives. The team should use the information to determine what progress the child made. If no progress can be established, the IEP team should take appropriate steps, including obtaining further assessment, to explain the child's lack of progress and propose changes to the IEP.

3. Parent Records

Parents of children with medical disabilities often possess or have access to voluminous records with essential information regarding the child's health needs while in school, information that should be shared with all members of the IEP team. While parent documentation alone cannot satisfy the school's obligation to obtain evaluation from persons qualified in the areas of the child's disability and appropriate services, parents can help the team to understand the disability and identify qualified professionals to further advise the team.

4. Teacher Records

Teacher information may be somewhat less important relative to health care related services as compared with instructional and other related service domains. Nevertheless, the teacher who works with the child should have regular communication with the related service provider to help that person assess the impact of interventions on the child's classroom functioning, interpret changes in the child's behavior, and adjust services as appropriate to help the child be more productive in the instructional process. The child's teacher thus has necessary information for the IEP team to consider in planning related services.

5. Related Service Records

If communication between the classroom teacher and the related service providers has been adequate, the records of this communication should help the IEP team work with the related service provider to develop strategies for the child to get the most benefit from instruction. If related service records are correlated with evaluative information and other information from the classroom, the IEP team participants should have a basis for recommending modifications to improve participation and quality of life.

III. WHO SHOULD BE PRESENT AT THE IEP TEAM MEETING TO CONSIDER MEDICAL SERVICES, AND WHY?

1. The Parent

The parent should be present as the representative of the child and the person who, under IDEA, has the right to speak for the child's interests. As indicated, parents of children with medical disabilities have essential information for the IEP team to consider. Parents of children with medical disabilities are often the best source of information for the IEP team as the team begins to consider health care related services for the child. These parents often have long contended with the child's disability and with health care professionals serving the child. They are probably familiar already with the kinds of tasks necessary to maintain the child's health status and the type of training needed to perform those tasks.

2. The Child's Special Education Teacher

The special education teacher should be present at the IEP team meeting to assist deliberations, particularly discussion of how the child's medical disability and the delivery of health care related services affect daily classroom functioning. If the special education teacher may be expected to implement health care procedures in the classroom, the teacher should be present at the meeting to help the team ascertain whether the teacher is qualified to implement those procedures and/or the extent of any training that may be necessary. The special education teacher will also have input in the design of health care IEP objectives, if any, that will be taught in the special education setting or with the assistance of special education.

3. The Child's Regular Education Teacher

If the child receives or may receive instruction in a general education setting, the child's general education teacher must attend the IEP team meeting. As with the special education teacher, the child's general education teacher has essential information about how the child's disability and the delivery of health care related services affect classroom functioning. Additionally, the general education teacher may need to be apprised of training requirements for necessary health care monitoring or procedures.

4. A School Administrator

An administrator or designee must attend the meeting as an official school representative with authority to commit the district's resources necessary to implement the IEP. The administrator may be the appropriate person to chair the IEP team, deferring as necessary to other team members with expertise regarding any health care services that may be the subject of discussion.

5. Health Care Specialists

Health care service providers involved in the supervision and delivery of the child's related services must have input to the IEP team regarding the related service itself, as well as any health care service or IEP objective in which school staff will be directly involved. Attending the IEP team meeting is one method for the provider to have this input, but, depending on the issues, written input or separate staffing or in-service sessions may be more effective. The important thing to remember is that the IEP team should have available at the IEP team meeting any and all information it needs to write appropriate IEP objectives and schedule related services that the school will be obligated to provide. Commentary to IDEA reauthorization contains language encouraging the participation of school health personnel in IEP team meetings.

6. Assessment Specialists

A person must be present at the IEP team meeting who can interpret any assessment results, including health-related assessments, that are relevant to the team's deliberations.

4. THE ORDER OF BUSINESS FOR IEP TEAM MEMBERS

1. The Chairperson

The person who conducts an IEP team meeting convened specifically to address health care IEP and/or related service should be a person having substantial background in the child's disability and, ideally, experience in the management of health care issues of children with medical disabilities in schools. This person usually will be a special education staff such as a supervisor, teacher, or appraisal specialist. This person needs to orchestrate the meeting to insure input from the parent and from other IEP team members with information relevant to the services in question. The chair-person must be able to create an atmosphere in which individuals with specialized and diverse backgrounds in both education and related service specialties can function as a team.

2. The Opening

After introductions, the chair should begin by summarizing the purpose of the meeting, indicating that the team will review assessment, objectives, and the related service health care issues raised by the parent or school staff. The chair should present the proposed order of presentations, including the parent and/or their representatives, the school district's representatives, and any invited consultants or other outside service providers. The chair should inquire if the parent is satisfied with the notice received concerning the timing and content of the meeting, understands the order of business, and has any request to alter the agenda, raise additional issues for consideration, or present additional matter to the team.

3. Presenting Evaluative Data

The IEP team must have available and consider current and accurate evaluative data, including functional educational and/or performance assessment in areas of the child's functioning affected by the medical or physical disability that requires health care related services or IEP objectives. If evaluative data are not sufficient to answer the relevant questions of team members, the team should consider ordering further assessment, and deferring further deliberations until current satisfactory data is available.

4. Identifying Present Performance

If the evaluative data are current and accurate, the team should elicit information from the child's teacher about the child's present performance in areas affected by the medical or physical disability. Depending on the nature and severity of the disability, this can include information about the child's alertness, vitality, and ability to function in the classroom setting, during transitions, and while being transported to and from school. The teacher should discuss relevant characteristics in health-related areas where the child might appropriately be expected to gain increased independence in self-monitoring and self-maintenance. Additionally, the providers of health care services and related services, or someone designated to serve as the proxy for these persons, should inform the IEP team regarding the child's characteristics and needs in the relevant areas.

5. Choosing Appropriate Services and Objectives

Based on current evaluative data and the input of the parent, instructional, and health care related service providers, the team is in a position to identify any appropriate objectives for the child's IEP and schedule the related services that are necessary for the child to benefit from special education.

6. Identifying Evaluation Procedures

The IEP team should follow the normal procedures for evaluating IEP health care skill objectives. Health care related service objectives that concern non-instructional services, such as respiratory care, nursing services, and the like, ordinarily will be evaluated by the professional with training and certification in the specialty area of that service. The role of special education in that case will be to monitor the impact of the service, if any, on the child's instructional program and to liaison with health care professionals and the parents as appropriate via informal communication or IDEA's formal procedures.

V. KEY DELIBERATIONS TO DOCUMENT

Any point that is worth serious discussion by the IEP team deserves mention in the written minutes of the team's deliberations. This is particularly true if the point is disputed or may be the subject of an appeal. If the team's decisions are questioned in a due process hearing, the written record can help to establish what the team discussed in the meeting even if the members later become unavailable or cannot remember what took place. The IEP team that considers health care related service issues will want to record several points. There should be at least a brief mention of the current assessment, the child's current eligibility, and the condition that establishes that eligibility. It will then be necessary for the record to reflect the relationship or link between the child's disability and the need for the related service. This establishes that the IEP team considered the first necessary prerequisite for authorizing the service. The record also should reflect an explanation of why the related service is "necessary" in order for the child to benefit from special education. For example, the service may be linked to an IEP objective, such as mastery of self-monitoring or self-care, or the service may be necessary simply to enable the child to be present and functioning in school in an acceptably safe manner. The record should reflect further that the team has determined that the service may be provided by a person who is not a physician, unless the service is purely for a diagnostic and evaluative purpose in which case the record should indicate that purpose. In any event, this documentation establishes the other elements of the health care related service standard.

Other issues may be helpful to document if a question arises among the IEP team members about the appropriateness of the service. One problem that may occur is a disagreement about the necessity of providing the service during school hours. This is an issue clearly that will need to be resolved by one or more of the specialized staff who work with the child in and outside of the school. Clinic doctors and nurses, for example, often do not have the training and experience to address educational issues competently, but they nevertheless make recommendations to parents and schools about special education issues. If communications break down, the IEP team may be forced to obtain a "second opinion" by another provider, or even take the issue to mediation or a due process hearing in which a hearing officer will have to make sense out of conflicting expert opinions. In either case, the disagreement among the team members will tend to be resolved faster and with less expense to the parties if the IEP team documents carefully its deliberations over why the team considers a particular service necessary or unnecessary and what evaluative data those deliberations are based on.

The training and qualifications of the school employee or agent who provides the service may become an issue. If so, the IEP team should identify the evaluative data that it relies upon in determining that person's qualifications. If a dispute develops, this documentation will help to establish that the team did give the matter consideration and relied on appropriate professional standards in identifying a qualified provider.

VI. INVOKING STOP-GAP MEASURES

As the reader should now be aware, the area of health care related services is fraught with opportunities for debate and disagreement and lacks well-defined and tested legal standards to guide decision making. The IEP team may recess the IEP meeting to consider health care related services in case of a dispute, or at any point the team feels further evaluative data is needed, or when additional documentation or references need to be reviewed or outside persons need to be consulted or invited to join the team. Often, a recess, possibly coupled with informal alternative dispute resolution, allows team members who are in disagreement to find alternatives that will resolve the impasse and produce an acceptable solution, as well as an appropriate IEP for the student.

Chapter 9

THE IEP MEETING TO ADDRESS ASSISTIVE TECHNOLOGY

I. BACKGROUND

The legal foundation for assistive technology devices and services is a relatively new addition to IDEA's edifice and one that greatly expands the potential obligation of public schools to fund services previously considered to be the responsibility of parents or other agencies. The IDEA federal definitions pertaining to assistive technology, which remain in place without change, place no limit on the type or nature of device or service that could be considered assistive technology. IDEA defines an assistive technology device to mean "any item, piece of equipment, or product system, whether acquired commercially off the shelf, modified, or customized, that is used to increase, maintain, or improve the functional capabilities of children with disabilities." And an assistive technology service is defined as "any service that directly assists a child with a disability in the selection, acquisition, or use of an assistive technology device." This includes: the evaluation of the needs of a child with a disability, including a functional evaluation of the child in the child's customary environment; purchasing, leasing, or otherwise providing for the acquisition of assistive technology devices by children with disabilities; selecting, designing, fitting, customizing, adapting, applying, retaining, repairing, or replacing assistive technology devices; coordinating and using other therapies, interventions, or services with assistive technology devices, such as those associated with existing education and rehabilitation plans and programs; training or technical assistance for a child with a disability or, if appropriate, that child's family; and training or technical assistance for professionals (including individuals providing education or rehabilitation services), employers,

129

or other individuals who provide services to, employ, or are otherwise substantially involved in the major life functions of children with disabilities.

As one observer quipped, this wide-open definition, read literally, includes renting a chauffeured limousine to transport a child to and from school the limousine being the assistive technology device and the chauffeur being the assistive technology service. However, Congress placed limits on the availability of assistive technology that would prevent this wasteful conclusion. Before a device or service will fall within the school's obligation to provide at no cost to the child or parent, the device or service must be necessary in order for the child to receive a free, appropriate public education. But, as it will become clear, the definition of necessity for related services is somewhat different than for other types of special education.

Under existing federal regulations, there are three ways under IDEA regulations that assistive technology might be necessary to provide FAPE. IDEA requires assistive technology devices or services to be available to the child "as a part of the child's (1) special education (2) related services or (3) supplementary aids and services. In other words, assistive technology must be necessary to implement the child's special education objectives and services successfully, necessary as part of a non-instructional service in order to enable the child to benefit from special education, or necessary to enable the child to be educated with non-disabled peers if that is otherwise appropriate. You may wish to refer to other chapters in this book to review the specific requirements for related services, special education methodology, and mainstreaming.

Although the language of existing regulations narrows considerably the availability of assistive technology according to educational necessity, there still remain many types of devices and services that schools could be required to provide that some believe should be the responsibility of other public agencies, if not the parent. To address this issue, the regulations make it clear that technology that is the legal obligation of another federal agency or program will not be suddenly transformed into the school's obligation by IDEA's assistive technology regulations. IDEA is not meant, for example, to displace other sources of funding under programs such as Medicaid and maternal child health. The school's obligation is to ensure that the assistive technology be made available at no cost to the parent whatever the ultimate funding source.

The school's ability to access private funding sources for assistive technology poses more difficult questions. Private health care insurance paid for by the parent or the parent's employer, for example, may entail a contractual obligation of the insurer to provide the child with certain types of devices and services, according to the terms of the insurance policy. If the insurance policy covers a device or service that falls within the federal definition of assistive technology and is necessary for the child to receive FAPE, the insurer should not necessarily be free to escape its contractual obligation to the child because of IDEA's publicly funded provision for the same device or service. Therefore, in principle, the public should not have to pay for what a private insurer already has contracted to provide.

Even if private insurance covers a necessary device or service, however, the school still may have to pay for the device or service. IDEA plainly requires that necessary assistive technology will be provided at no cost to the parent. If drawing upon private health insurance causes the parent to have to pay a higher premium, lose coverage, lose access to future benefits, or incur any other cost out of pocket, there would be a violation of IDEA's economic protection for parents. In that case, it would not be permissible for the school to look to private insurance to cover the cost of the device or service.

Despite the specter of limitless school liability for assistive technology devices and services, examination of recent IDEA-related legal decisions that raise substantial technology related issues uncovers no great volume of litigation in this area. Indeed, there is seemingly no more litigation over assistive technology than in other controversial areas such as discipline and LRE. The fact that schools and parents are not litigating many assistive technology issues to hearing may mean that either parents are preferring to keep control over the prescription and delivery of technology devices by obtaining the devices themselves or else schools are being successful in finding alternative funding sources.

Legal inquiry nevertheless has helped to address some important areas. At one time, for example, considerable controversy surrounded school officials' efforts to distinguish "personal" or non-educational devices, such as glasses and hearing aids that the child would require regardless of whether the child was in school or not, from assistive technology necessary for educational purposes. The guidance from OSEP has been somewhat helpful in this controversy. It appears that districts are not obligated to provide technology that the child requires for non-educational purposes. However, if this same technology also is necessary for the child to receive educational benefit, the school must provide it even if the child also requires it for non-educational purposes.

It is difficult to imagine, and the case law does not help to distinguish, what type of assistive technology device or service a child might require for non-educational reasons that would not also be necessary for FAPE. Hearing aids, eye-glasses, computer-assisted communication devices, and even wheelchairs or devices to assist ambulation likely could be linked to a valid and necessary educational objective for the child. OSEP has opined that hearing aids, eyeglasses, and even a pulmonary nebulizer used to administer medication necessary during the school day can be required assistive technology devices. So, reliance on the "personal device" distinction is not helpful. The only real inquiry in a disagreement over assistive technology is whether the device is truly necessary in order for the child to receive FAPE. If it is necessary, the school must insure that it is provided and paid for by some funding source that involves no cost to the child or parent. This is why qualified assistive technology assessment is essential.

Another type of dispute has focused on the qualifications of personnel to assess assistive technology needs, to use the technology itself with the child, or to instruct the child in using assistive technology. State agency guidelines for the certification or hiring of assistive technology specialists can help the school and the parent identify the type of person who is qualified to conduct an assessment. If the school or parent expects a dispute to arise regarding assessment of the child's needs, then it would be wise to pay special attention to the qualifications of the assessment person chosen, since that person may have to testify in support of proposed technology, and expert witness credibility turns substantially on past training, experience and other qualifications. The assessment specialist should have a broad background in special education, including assessment techniques and instructional methods for the child's particular disability, as well as training and experience in use of the proposed technology with that type of disability. When special qualifications are needed for the staff who will actually use the technology for instructional purposes, the school and parent must attend to the appropriate training of instructional staff, and the parent, if necessary, as an assistive technology service. An expert with experience in the technology will be the most appropriate person to outline special training requirements, if any, for instructional staff.

The Foundation: Proper Use of Assessment

Issues involving assistive technology create no exception to the general rule that assessment is the starting point for determining the necessity of technology devices and services. A public agency must evaluate a student in all areas of suspected disability, including whether a student requires the use of assistive technology devices or services. Furthermore, a parent's right to an independent educational evaluation includes an assessment that will enable an IEP team to determine the student's assistive technology needs. The right to an IEE arises when the school neglects to evaluate the student for assistive technology needs or when the parent disagrees with the school's evaluation of assistive technology needs. A parent also can request that the school conduct a reevaluation of the student's need for assistive technology.

The child's comprehensive individual assessment, which will include assessment of assistive technology needs, is the starting point for questions concerning assistive technology devices and services. Before the school becomes obligated to provide assistive technology, the assistive device or service must be necessary in order for the child to benefit from special education as a related service necessary as an aspect of the child's instruction as special education, or necessary in order for the child to function successfully in the general education setting as a supplementary aid or service.

Oddly enough, according to OSEP's recent reading of the assistive technology regulations, assistive technology may be necessary even if the need for the technology is not related to the child's IDEA disability. Recall that the regulations say assistive technology may be required *as a part of* the eligible child's special instruction, related service, or supplementary aids and services. The regulations do not expressly require that the technology be needed just to correct or compensate for the child's specific IDEA disability. According to OSEP, the only relevant inquiry for the IEP team is whether the device is necessary as part of special education, related service, or supplementary aids and services, in order for the child to receive FAPE. Therefore, the relationship between the technology and the disability may not be the dispositive issue, if the IEP team finds that the disabled child cannot receive FAPE without the device, and includes it in the child's IEP.

So, for example, if a learning disabled child required corrective lenses in order to participate in his resource class, benefit from O.T., or use certain instructional modifications in the general education classroom, the school would be obligated to ensure that the child was provided glasses at no cost to the parent. While special education, related services, and supplementary aids and services ordinarily are required only to address domains affected by the child's IDEA disability, OSEP's interpretation seems to make an exception to this general rule for assistive technology.

Identifying Present Performance, Goals, and Objectives

In making assistive technology decisions, the IEP team should consider (1) whether the technology or service itself requires specific objectives of its own and (2) what, if any, IEP objectives and/or appropriate general education curriculum objectives are supported by the technology. To the extent that goals and objectives are present, they should be specified in objective and measurable terms and should have their own methods and schedule for evaluation.

Assistive technology devices that are an aspect of special instruction or integral to functioning in general education, for example, communications software, communications hardware, self-organization software, and the like, may be complex and difficult enough for the child to use. Furthermore, this technology itself may actually be a substitute method of performing a major life activity whose normal performance is affected by the disability reading, writing, speaking, etc. With technology of this nature, learning to use the device is tantamount to learning to perform the major life activity. If so, it would be inappropriate to introduce the technology to the child without the same general kinds of objectives and strategies, for using the technology itself, that would be required to teach the activity to children who do not have the disability! When this is the case, the IEP team should rely on experts with knowledge of the technology to help develop appropriate objectives and strategies congruent with the team's knowledge of the whole child, and to help develop evaluation methods. If this were not required as special education, it would most likely be required as an assistive technology service.

If the assistive technology does not require its own goals and objectives, it will be important for the IEP team to link the technology to appropriate objectives in the child's IEP or to some objectives in the general education curriculum. That is critical to insure that the IEP team carefully considers the relevance of the technology and its potential educational impact. Objectives affected by technology should have a statement of the present performance level or characteristics, a measurable, behavioral statement of the objective itself, and a method and timetable for evaluating progress on the objective.

In most published cases where assistive technology has been the central issue of litigation, technology is almost always alleged necessary to address appropriate educational objectives where it can be shown that the child has failed to make progress without the technology. If a child is failing to progress, the party proposing use of the technology has almost a presumption favoring the use of the technology, so long as credible expert testimony is offered to establish that the technology will correct the child's failure. Conversely, cases show that the party opposing the use of a proposed technology can prevail by showing that the child already is making meaningful progress without the technology, on educational objectives for which the technology is thought to be essential by the party proposing it.

The IEP team always has a difficult burden when a child with a disability fails to make educational progress. The best available expertise often is insufficient to pinpoint the exact cause of the child's failure, and the team may have to struggle with strongly diverging views of what new intervention will fix the problem. Occasionally, in these situations someone proposes a technology device or service as a "quick fix" for the child's problem and the team impulsively follows, but no improvement occurs. That is why it is particularly important to have current assistive technology assessment that is integrated with other comprehensive assessment and evaluative data to identify the options likely to be successful for the child. It is even more important to have a clear picture of present performance, as well as goals and objectives, telling the team where the child should be headed educationally. Without proper assessment and appropriate goals, the school may well end up wasting money on costly devices that ultimately do not benefit the child. More importantly, the child has wasted valuable instructional time that might better have been spent on a different approach.

Choosing the Least Restrictive Educational Environment

Parties occasionally allege that even though the child is already making progress in a more restrictive environment, the addition of some assistive technology would enable the child to make progress in a general education setting or at least increase the amount of time the child though the child is already receiving meaningful benefit, the liberal standard for assistive technology can result in the school having to provide the technology as supplementary aids and services for the primary purpose of increasing mainstreaming.

When technology is proposed mainly to increase mainstreaming, the team should be careful to develop an independent justification for the mainstreaming itself, using the guidelines described in a preceding chapter. Studying the child's present performance, goals, and current assessment tells the IEP team whether and to what extent the general education curriculum is appropriate for the child, and whether the child can benefit from noneducational social experiences in the mainstream, in order to increase the child's competence and independence. The cart should not be leading the horse here. Ask first whether additional mainstreaming will be appropriate for the child and, then, whether technology can help realize that.

II. WHAT DOCUMENTATION SHOULD THE TEAM HAVE AVAILABLE TO CONSIDER, AND WHY?

1. The Most Recent Comprehensive Individual Assessment

It is essential to have current comprehensive assessment that specifically addresses assistive technology in light of the child's current physical, developmental, language, and learning characteristics, as well as estimated short and long-term goals. Without this comprehensive perspective, the IEP team cannot properly evaluate the need for devices that intrinsically affect the child's level of independence and autonomy, either positively or negatively.

2. The Most Recent IEP Documents

If the child is receiving special education services, the IEP team should examine the last IEP documents for the statement of present performance, as well as the last set of goals and objectives. Information about the child's progress, which can be obtained by comparing the child's present performance against the last IEP objectives, is highly relevant to determining the need, if any, for assistive technology. If the child is not making progress, the IEP team must consider the possibility that the child may require new or different assistive technology.

3. Parent Records

Parents of children with disabilities often are motivated to search for and have access to specialized networks that provide documentation regarding new technological advances that may help their child in school. Thus, parents often have valuable documentation for the IEP team regarding assistive technology. The team should always consider documentation from the parent.

4. Teacher Records

Records from the child's classroom teacher in general education and special education classes are essential to establish present performance and, therefore, progress in the general education curriculum and/or special education IEP objectives. Teacher documentation, such as grades, test scores, test documents, workbooks, assignments, and other work product of the student, is the most credible source of information about the child's performance and progress. This information, as explained, goes to the heart of the determination regarding necessity of assistive technology. The classroom teacher also has the insights gained from weeks of daily work with the child, which can shed light on the child's ability to use and benefit from assistive technology. This information relates directly to the child's need for assistive technology as part of special education or as part of supplementary aids and services in the regular classroom.

5. Related Service Records

Since assistive technology may be necessary as a part of related services, the assessment and input of the related service provider is essential to determining the need for assistive technology in this area.

III. WHO SHOULD BE PRESENT AT THE IEP TEAM MEETING TO CONSIDER ASSISTIVE TECHNOLOGY, AND WHY?

1. The Parent

The parent should be present as the representative of the child and the person who, under IDEA, has the right to speak for the child's interests. Parents of children with disabilities usually are highly motivated to search for new technological advances that may help their child in school. They may have time, resources, and access to specialized networks in the technology arena that school professionals do not. Thus, parents often have valuable documentation for the IEP team regarding assistive technology. The team should always consider information that the parent presents in this area, as in other areas of IEP development.

2. The Child's Special Education Teacher

If the child is receiving special education services, the special education teacher should be present at the IEP team meeting to assist the deliberations regarding present performance, the child's present educational benefit, and the need for assistive technology as part of special education.

3. The Child's Regular Education Teacher

If the child receives or may receive instruction in a general education setting, the child's general education teacher or teachers must attend the IEP team meeting to address assistive technology. The decisions that the IEP team will make regarding technology are likely to have long-range and far reaching impact on the child's education, which makes the mainstream teacher's presence essential. If a particular regular education teacher cannot be the teacher present during the IEP team meeting, the teacher should be briefed beforehand on the assistive technology device or service that will be discussed at the meeting, and should have input via written report or proxy regarding the likely impact of the technology on the child's functioning in the general education classroom. If technology is proposed because of the child's failure in the general education setting, the teacher should offer his or her opinion, if any, about the reason for the child's failure, and the relevance of the proposed technology to remediating the specific problem or problems.

4. A School Administrator

An administrator or designee must attend the meeting as an official school representative with authority to commit the district's resources necessary to implement the IEP. The administrator may be the appropriate person to chair the IEP team, deferring as necessary to other team members with expertise regarding assessment and assistive technology issues.

5. Assessment Specialists

The IEP team must include an assessment specialist who is qualified to give the team an overview of any assessment that has been completed on the child. This person has the job of explaining and interpreting the current assessment, and showing how assistive technology fits the child's unique pattern of strengths and educational needs. This person should communicate before the IEP team meeting with any assistive technology specialist or consultant who is working with the child in order to inform the assistive technology specialist, and to understand the assistive technology recommendations. A person must be present at the IEP team meeting who can interpret any specific assessment results relevant to the team's deliberations.

6. Assistive Technology Specialists

Persons qualified in assessment and planning for assistive technology must have input at the meeting to consider assistive technology. Long before the meeting, the assistive technology specialist should have met the child, reviewed current assessment results from physical, psychomotor, intellectual, behavioral, and academic domains, interviewed the child's teachers and the assessment specialist, and interviewed the parent, using the information gained thereby to plan interventions appropriate to the child's needs. The assistive technology specialist ideally should attend the IEP team meeting. However, if the aforementioned background work has been done beforehand, the assistive technology specialist is more likely to confer with the parents and school professionals before the team meeting regarding the necessity of any technology and submit a report for the team's consideration. If the background work has not been done and the specialist does not attend the IEP team meeting, both the school and the specialist could be in for some difficult moments in a later hearing or deposition as the specialist struggles to explain their choice of technology without knowing the child, and the school's IEP team members try to explain why they relied on an inadequate assessment!

IV. THE ORDER OF BUSINESS FOR IEP TEAM MEMBERS

1. The Chairperson

Ideally, the person who conducts an IEP team meeting convened specifically to address assistive technology should have substantial background in the child's disability, along with experience and training in either assistive technology or assessment. This person usually will be a special education supervisor or appraisal specialist. This person needs to orchestrate the meeting to insure input from the parent and from other IEP team members with information relevant to the technology in question. The chair-person must be able to create an atmosphere in which individuals with specialized and diverse backgrounds in both education and technology speciality areas can function as a team.

2. The Opening

Following introductions, the chair should introduce the participants if they have not met, and summarize the purpose of the meeting, indicating that the team will review assessment, IEP objectives, and the assistive technology issues raised by the parent or by school staff. The chair should indicate the proposed order of presentations, including the parent and/or their representatives, the school district's representatives, and any invited consultants or specialists. The chair should inquire if the parent is satisfied with the notice received concerning the timing and content of the meeting, understands the order of business, and has any request to alter the agenda, raise additional issues for consideration, or present additional matter to the team.

3. Presenting Evaluative Data

The IEP team must have available and must consider current and accurate evaluative data, including assessment and evaluative data pertaining to the child's assistive technology needs. This includes data about the child's present performance in areas that may be affected by the proposed use of assistive technology. If evaluative data are not sufficient to answer the relevant questions of team members, the team should consider ordering further assessment and deferring further deliberations until current satisfactory data is available.

4. Identifying Present Performance

The team should obtain information from the child's teacher about the child's present performance in areas that may be affected by the proposed assistive technology. Hopefully, this information will include not only the teacher's oral report but also tangible proof such as work samples, tests, grade sheets, and the like. Teacher data regarding present performance helps focus the team on the specific educational need that will justify either providing the proposed assistive technology or choosing some other approach. Without current assessment and evaluation of present performance, both academic and social, the task of choosing technology becomes an impossible one. For example, a child who is far below his grade placement with respect to academic skills will probably not benefit from general education classes for academics, even with a device that improves his ability to communicate with adults and peers. The device may, however, assist appropriate mainstreaming in other areas where the child can receive social and behavioral benefit from increased interaction. Another example might be the child with a disability in written expression for whom a laptop computer and spelling checker is requested to complete written assignments. If the child is still developing and showing progress with respect to his unaided handwriting and spelling skills, the computer might interfere with achievement of written language goals essential for the child's personal independence, even though providing a short-term solution to a perceived problem. An integrated assistive technology assessment can help the IEP team avoid pitfalls and false promises offered by the growing array of new devices and services.

5. Choosing Appropriate Technology

After receiving and considering current evaluative data input from the parent, teachers, assessment specialist, and assistive technology specialist, the team should now be in a position to determine what educational objectives are appropriate for the child, which of those objectives, if any, justify the use of proposed assistive technology, and how the technology is necessary for the child to make progress on those objectives. If the technology itself is necessary for the child to perform some major life activity, the IEP should set out any educational concerns regarding the use of the technology. For example, if the technology requires instruction before the child can benefit from it, or if the technology is a substitute for the normal development of some life activity such as oral communication, the technology itself will require appropriate objectives that fit in with the child's long range educational goals and/or transition goals. Similarly, if the technology is proposed mainly in order to increase the child's ability to participate in general education, the IEP must specify how the technology will accomplish that aim and should include any objectives to support the use of the technology. In choosing appropriate technology, the team cannot overlook the essential task of providing necessary assistive technology services in the IEP to support the technology. Typically, services might include training of instructional and other educational staff, the child, and the parent, regarding appropriate use and maintenance of the technology.

6. Identifying Evaluation Procedures

The IEP team should follow the normal procedures for evaluating IEP objectives that either pertain directly to the implementation of the technology itself or are thought to be affected by the technology's use. Such evaluative data are required by current regulations but more importantly, will form the basis upon which the IEP team makes subsequent decisions regarding the assistive technology.

V. KEY DELIBERATIONS TO DOCUMENT

Any point that is worth serious discussion by the IEP team deserves mention in the written minutes of the team's deliberations. This is particularly true if the point is disputed or may be the subject of an appeal. If the team's decisions are questioned in a due process hearing, the written record can help to establish what the team discussed in the meeting even if the members later become unavailable or cannot remember what took place. The key issues to discuss and document with respect to assistive technology concern how the technology is necessary as part of special education, related service, or supplementary aids and services, in order for the child to receive FAPE. The team will always need to document its awareness and understanding of the child's special education assessment, eligibility, and handicapping condition. At the same time, since the relationship between the technology and the disability is not the only issue in discussing assistive technology, the team will need to discuss and document that it has considered all the ways that assistive technology might assist the child to receive FAPE whether as part of special education, related services, or supplementary aids and services to support mainstreaming. This includes possible FAPE-related benefits of assistive technology that are not necessarily directly related to the child's disability.

Since assistive technology can give rise to disputes about staff qualifications, which implicates assistive technology services, it will be essential for the IEP team to document that it has made appropriate inquiry regarding what training and expertise are necessary to make use of the technology. The team also must document the steps that will be taken to obtain necessary staff and/or parent training, as well as training for the child. Clearing up these questions during the IEP team meeting can save a lot of trouble if a question arises later and it appears that no one on the team considered special training needs.

The commencement date for a technology device or service may become important, where technology is difficult to obtain or where steps must be taken administratively to allocate necessary funds. The IEP team should demonstrate that it has considered delivery issues regarding necessary technology, estimated a realistic commencement date, and addressed ways of compensating for any FAPE problem that might arise because of such issues.

VI. INVOKING STOP-GAP MEASURES

The federal assistive technology regulations create a fairly liberal standard in favor of providing various forms of technology to support special education. While the frequency of disputes between schools and parents in this area does not appear to be overwhelming, the IEP team still should be aware of the option to recess the IEP meeting to consider disputed assistive technology issues, particularly when the team believes that further evaluative data is needed, or when additional documentation or references need to be reviewed or outside persons need to be consulted or invited to join the team.

Chapter 10

THE IEP MEETING TO ADDRESS
REIMBURSEMENT FOR PRIVATE SERVICES

I. BACKGROUND

In the 1985 case of *Burlington School Committee v. Massachusetts Department of Education,* the U.S. Supreme Court affirmed that public schools can be ordered to reimburse the parent of a disabled child for the cost of a private school placement by the parent, when a court concludes both that the public school system failed to provide the child a free, appropriate public education and that the private school chosen by the parents did provide an appropriate education. The Court reasoned that IDEA was not meant to require parents to "go along with the IEP to the detriment of their child if it turns out to be inappropriate or pay for what they consider to be the appropriate placement." If parents choose the private placement at their own expense because the public school's program is not appropriate, then the public school should have to reimburse those private school expenses.

IDEA now expressly authorizes reimbursement for private services in certain situations where the school has failed to provide or cannot provide an appropriate IEP and the parents have followed IDEA's notice procedures. IDEA does not specifically require that the private services deliver FAPE in order to be reimbursed, but common sense dictates that schools should not be required to reimburse inappropriate private services, and IDEA reauthorization did not expressly override *Burlington* in this regard. The following discussion assumes that both prongs of the *Burlington* standard remain viable in analyzing reimbursement claims.

It is well, settled case law that a public school may have to reimburse the parents for past private tutoring, private related services, or full-time attendance at a private school, if the public school denies the child FAPE and those private services are necessary for, and do in fact deliver, FAPE. Public schools also can be required to reimburse even a private *residential* placement by the parent, or at least the educational, psychosocial, and maintenance costs of that placement, if the school district cannot provide FAPE, and the parents can prove both that residential placement is necessary for the child to receive an appropriate education and that the specific residential facility in question delivers FAPE. As some judges have formulated the issue, residential placement, as the placement of last resort, may be required when the child's IDEA disability is "inextricably intertwined" with the behaviors and/or deficits that make public school education not feasible.

However, in deciding a question of whether reimbursement is proper, the decision maker should not try to balance out the relative benefits of the public school's program against the program offered by the private placement. The threshold question is whether the public school's program is appropriate. That question is not answered by comparing programs. If the public school's IEP delivers an appropriate program, the public school is not obligated to reimburse the parents for their private placement, even if the private placement appears "better."

Cases that have concerned a parent's right to reimbursement for private services spell out the issues that schools, parents, and IEP teams must heed before risking costly conflict over reimbursement for private services. Typically, parents who seek reimbursement for private placement in the *past* must show in retrospect that the school's past program was inappropriate. This means proving that the child was not making meaningful progress in the school's program and the school's deficient IEP and/or services were the reason why.

Parents or school officials prospectively seeking *future* private placement at public expense must show that the school has historically been unable to educate the child in a way that provides meaningful benefit and that the school, using educational services and related services available to it, is not likely to be able to educate the child successfully during the future time period for which reimbursement is sought. Whether a party seeks reimbursement for past or prospective private placement, the party also must show that the private placement can provide, or did provide, a FAPE for the child. To paraphrase one judge's summary, it is necessary to show not only that public school's IEP methods failed but also that the outside program will work for the child.

New IDEA notice provisions require that parents seeking reimbursement first notify the public school ten days in advance of their intent to do so. This requirement reduces the "trial by ambush" tactic adopted by some attorneys who advised parents to withdraw their children from public school, enroll them in private school, and immediately request due process to have the public school pay private tuition. Now, the public school has an opportunity to conduct an IEP meeting attempting to modify the public school's program to correct IEP deficiencies. If parents fail to provide this notice before making a reimbursement claim in the due process forum, they risk denial of their claim and reduction of attorney's fee reimbursement as well.

Parents seeking reimbursement for residential placement, or schools seeking to compel residential placement, bear a heavy burden to demonstrate the appropriateness of such placement because it is one of the most restrictive options available on the continuum of services. Judges are reluctant to order residential placement under IDEA's standards because the residential placement typically offers no opportunity, or extremely limited opportunity, for the child to interact with non-disabled peers. Furthermore, many experts believe that residential placements tend to adapt children to a sheltered, highly supervised, externally directed life-style. This makes it difficult to plan and implement transition services for independent or semi-independent living, assuming independent living is otherwise an appropriate transition goal for the child. However, for children whose emotional, cognitive, or other disability characteristics make progress in the public schools virtually impossible, residential placement may be the only option.

Recurring Issues in Reimbursement Cases

The following paragraphs will highlight some of the recurring factual patterns in reimbursement cases, and their implications, where parents have sought public reimbursement of private services. As indicated before, one prerequisite for obtaining reimbursement of private services is a showing that the child's public school IEP is or was inappropriate. Problems with the IEP that have led to reimbursement orders may be classified as *procedural problems*, and *substantive problems*. This classification flows from the Supreme Court's analysis, in *Board of Education v. Rowley,* of the school's obligation with respect to IEP development, which is that (1) the IEP must be developed in accordance with

IDEA's procedures and (2) the IEP must be reasonably calculated to enable the child to receive meaningful educational benefit.

Examining the Public School Program - Is It Providing FAPE?

Procedural Defects. Educators occasionally forget that *procedural* defects in the IEP process alone can lead to a finding that the IEP is inappropriate, at least if those defects interfered with the development of an appropriate IEP or with parent participation. This finding, in turn, can open the door for the public school to reimburse private tuition or services for the time in which an inappropriate IEP was in effect. This book's purpose is not to review IDEA's specific procedural requirements. It is nevertheless important to note here certain procedural flaws that have, alone or in combination with other factors supported a finding that an IEP was inappropriate leading to reimbursement for private services.

Keep in mind that there is not always a fine line between what may be considered procedural and what may be considered substantive. For example, the IEP team's failure to receive and discuss current assessment and other evaluative data could be considered procedural, though obviously this affects the substantive decisions made by the IEP team. The common themes in the procedural flaw decisions suggest procedural errors may be fatal to the IEP when they either cause the development of an inappropriate IEP or interfere with the parent's ability to participate fully in the IEP process. Here are some procedural problems described in case law.

Assessment

- the comprehensive assessment was out of date or not completed within required time lines;
- the child's present performance was not identified in objective terms;
- the comprehensive assessment was based on flawed testing;
- the school failed to assess the child in areas where known facts indicated a suspected disability.

IEP Process:

- the public school failed to develop annual IEP in a timely fashion, because IEP was out of date at beginning of school year;

- the IEP team failed obtain adequate and current evaluative data before writing IEP;
- the IEP did not contain all required components;
- the child's teacher was not present at the IEP team meeting;
- the public school staff familiar with all placement options that might be appropriate for the child were not present at the IEP meeting;
- representatives of a private school proposed by the parent were not invited or present at the IEP meeting;
- the child's IEP objectives were too vague to be understandable;
- the IEP team failed to discuss and/or to address disabilities and educational needs identified in the child's comprehensive assessment;
- the behavior management plan was generic, not individualized;
- the IEP team failed to discuss and specify the relationship between the child's disability and the choice of educational strategies;
- the public school failed or refused to consider changing educational methodology despite child's persistent failure;
- the public school failed to deliver all services scheduled in IEP;
- public school representatives decided the child's placement before writing the IEP, and failed to consider LRE;
- the public school failed to include evaluation in the IEP and failed to conduct evaluation of progress on IEP objectives.

PARENT PARTICIPATION/NOTICE:

- the public school failed to provide the parent with timely, accurate notice regarding IEP team meetings;
- the public school failed to provide notice and explanation of reasons for refusing the parent's reimbursement request;
- the public school denied a parent request to have input at the IEP team meeting;
- the public school failed to consider all proposed placement options, including the parent's proposal for private facility;
- the public school staff changed the child's placement before convening IEP team meeting.

Substantive defects. Substantive, as opposed to procedural, problems with the IEP lead to public school reimbursement for private services when those problems deny FAPE. There obviously are a great many ways that an IEP can be substantively deficient, and it is not the aim of this book to catalog all possible deficiencies. It may, however, be useful to consider some of the IEP problems described in legal opinions in cases where the public school has been ordered to reimburse private services or a private placement. Members of the IEP team, prior to and during the IEP meeting to consider reimbursement for private placement or services, must be alert to the existence of one or more of these kinds of problems.

Goals and Objectives

- the IEP omitted annual goals and short-term objectives that had been included in previous IEPs but not mastered;
- the IEP objectives were too vague for parents to understand, or instructional staff to implement;
- IEP goals and objectives contradicted the child's assessed learning characteristics and assessment recommendations;
- the IEP team failed to recognize obvious signs of the student's emotional problems, and failed to address them by considering or increasing counseling, and/or developing a behavior management plan;
- the IEP team identified the existence of a learning disability but failed to develop the child's IEP with that diagnosis in mind.

Placement/LRE

- the IEP provided excessive mainstreaming - general education classes utilized concepts and language that were much more complex than the child could handle;
- the public school changed the child's educational placement and LRE without an IEP team meeting;
- the public school's proposed special education placement was presented to the parent without any proposed IEP objectives and services.

Special Education and Related Services

- the IEP did not include adequate services to afford the child a reasonable opportunity to achieve his annual goals;
- the student failed to make year-for-year progress in academic skills, when assessment data indicated such progress would have been appropriate;

- the special education team failed to monitor the student's progress, including difficulties in regular education classes where the student was failing;
- public school staff drafted temporary "transitional" IEPs that omitted important details necessary for the student's educational program;
- public school staff failed to consider changed circumstances that indicated the need for assessment and additional services.

Methodology

- the public school addressed the mainstreamed student's persistent failure by increasing special education time, despite having previously decreased it to bolster the student's self-esteem, but failed to consider changing the instructional methodology.

Can Public Schools Ever *Deliver FAPE?*

The long and growing list of potential procedural and substantive problems, which pose liability risks for public schools and FAPE risks for children, suggests to some parents and educators alike that there is no practical way to feel confident about the appropriateness of special education services. Educators in particular sometimes react with hopelessness, passivity, or misplaced anger toward parents and special education lawyers. Even in areas where educators are supposed to have discretion because of their expertise, such as methodology choice, judges sometimes impose liability on schools if it appears the child is not making meaningful progress.

In this particular context, it seems worth mentioning that millions if IEPs are written every year, but only a very small fraction of these lead to impartial due process hearings. In those that do, judges frequently forgive minor procedural or substantive flaws when the school is aware and responding to the student's needs in a flexible way, and the student is making progress consistent with his or her estimated learning potential. Given the variety and severity of disabilities that special educators deal with and the lack of "hard" data regarding methodology, the success rate of special education seems astounding. Anger and resentment toward IDEA's due process rights is disproportionate to the real impact of IDEA's procedures. Millions of American students with disabilities are being educated successfully, and even greater numbers of parents are effective participants in the IEP process and satisfied public school customers.

Examining the Private Services - Do They Deliver FAPE?

When the child's parent requests a private service, the IEP team, as a procedural mater, must *consider* that request. Recall, though, that reimbursement is only appropriate when (1) the public school program does not or cannot deliver FAPE *and* (2) the private school provides an appropriate program. Assuming, for purposes of discussion here, it is assumed that the IEP team does consider a proposed private placement or service because it has already investigated and decided there are fatal flaws in the public school's past program, or that the public school cannot feasibly deliver an appropriate program for some time in the future. What factors will be relevant for the team to consider in evaluating the private service? How does the IEP team go about considering whether the parent is entitled to reimbursement? Published opinions suggest some of the factors or circumstances that the IEP team should consider in cases where it is necessary to examine the private school program carefully in order to determine whether it is appropriate.

Were the services provided by the private placement appropriate? Before the IEP team considers reimbursing private services, the team should investigate the private program or service and make its own determination that these are appropriate and beneficial for the child. A private program is not obligated to meet all of IDEA's procedural requirements or to document assessment and services in the same way as the public school. The private program or service nevertheless must be backed up by some evidence that the child has measurably benefitted from appropriate services (for reimbursement of prior services), or that the child can reasonably be expected to benefit in the future from the private program or service (for reimbursement of future services). This evidence will need to be substantial in order to survive scrutiny if the matter ends up in an impartial due process hearing. The public school's representatives on the IEP team would be foolish to reject a parent request for private services out of hand without first studying the appropriateness of the private program as well as their own program.

Specific deficiencies in *private* programs or services have been duly noted by reviewing judges in cases where reimbursement was denied because of the private program's inappropriateness. Here are some deficiencies that have caused problems for the private programs in reimbursement cases:

Individualized Program or Service

- the private program did not have program tailored specifically to child's individual needs;
- the private program failed to provide individualized services that were necessary for the child, e.g. counseling;
- the private school program lacked any individualized instructional goals and objectives;
- the private program's goals and/or services failed to address the child's identified disability.

Special Quality of Instruction or Services

- the private program was not substantially different from public school program;
- the private program provided methodologies that were not appropriate;
- the private program offered larger classes and less individualized attention than the public school program;
- the teaching staff of the private program lacked training, experience, and/or expertise in methods necessary to address the child's disability.

Benefit to the Child in the LRE

- the child failed to make progress on academic and/or behavioral goals in the private program;
- the private program offered few or no opportunities for the child to interact with non-disabled peers.

Are the costs of the private program or service reasonable? Even if the private program's services are appropriate, the important q u e s - tion remains whether the costs of the private program are reasonable. Judges have refused to award reimbursement for a private placement whose costs were excessive. The comparison often is made between the cost of the proposed private placement or service, and some objective data about the "average" or "typical" cost of comparable private services, based on available records concerning private services previously reimbursed by the state or public school district. Public schools that have already agreed to fund private placements at a reasonable or typical cost have succeeded in avoiding alternative, inordinately expensive placement proposed by the parent, by showing that a less costly program offered, or will offer, FAPE. But keep in mind, where the public school has failed to offer an appropriate program, the public school may have an uphill battle avoiding reimbursement on grounds of excessive cost, unless the public school offered an alternative *private* program that was both appropriate and less expensive.

Of course, if the public school's own program was appropriate in the past and/or the public school offers its own appropriate program in the future, then a reimbursement claim against the public school will likely fail. And a student's prior success with a particular program, approach, methodology, or mix of services is usually the best evidence of an appropriate program and the best gauge of what is likely to succeed in the future.

The Decision Making Process

II. WHAT DOCUMENTATION SHOULD THE TEAM HAVE AVAILABLE TO CONSIDER, AND WHY?

1. The Most Recent Comprehensive Individual Assessment

Because the current CIA is the foundation of FAPE, the IEP team will need to reference the CIA in the crucial determination of whether the public school's program has been appropriate. This is why it matters a great deal whether members of the IEP team all agree that the existing assessment is current and appropriate or whether some team members dispute the accuracy and/or timeliness of the assessment.

If, at the very outset, a team member challenges the appropriateness of the CIA itself, the team first must resolve disagreement among its members regarding appropriate assessment, possibly by obtaining further assessment if necessary. Ideally, the team should reach consensus on a single assessment and proceed from there. If the team is not able to reach consensus on a single assessment, for example, if the public school representatives have decided to litigate a parent request for independent evaluation, then resolution of the reimbursement issue becomes more complicated, from both a professional and a procedural standpoint.

A special education impartial hearing officer may be reluctant to decide the reimbursement issue without first resolving an assessment dispute by either obtaining stipulated agreement on an assessment or litigating the assessment disputes to a decision. Of course, if the assessment is found appropriate as a result of a hearing, the hearing officer can go on to examine the IEP that was based on that assessment and decide if it, too, is appropriate. Otherwise, the scenario changes.

Here is one example. If the public school's assessment is found inappropriate at the hearing and the IEP team based previous IEPs on that inappropriate assessment, then those IEPs themselves might be inappropriate. If the parent requests reimbursement for past private services because of alleged deficiencies in those IEPs and the hearing officer finds the IEPs inappropriate because of the inappropriate assessments, then the parent has cleared the major hurdle in obtaining reimbursement. As a practical matter, both a prior assessment and a prior IEP might be tested in the same due process hearing. Resolution of the assessment issue would precede a determination of reimbursement for challenged IEPs from the past.

In a different example, the dispute might concern an IEP scheduled for implementation in the future, with the parent seeking reimbursement prospectively because of a disagreement with some part of an IEP based on current assessment. This tends to create a dilemma for hearing officers if they understand the central role of assessment in the IEP process. The hearing officer first has to decide if the assessment is appropriate, which may require a due process hearing. If the assessment is found inappropriate, the hearing officer normally must order a new assessment, often an IEE, which must occur before making further decisions about the IEP. Since hearing officers normally do not use the hearing process to write IEP, there must be an IEP team meeting to consider the new assessment and an IEP written that addresses the new assessment findings. Only then is the reimbursement claim, based on the appropriateness of the public school's IEP, "ripe" for decision.

Considering these examples, one can see that very different consequences can result from the IEP team's deliberations about assessment when considering the issue of reimbursement of private services that the school or parent proposes. These complications do, however, serve to illustrate, in yet another way, the essential role of assessment in building the foundation for an appropriate IEP.

For now, we will assume that the IEP team has current, appropriate assessment, and has used that assessment to write an IEP that is now in dispute. The IEP team must proceed to study that IEP carefully from the perspective of the current assessment findings and to determine the fate of disputed portions of the IEP that allegedly are so inappropriate as to require reimbursement for private services. In this process, the team may find that it is necessary or advisable to consider a specific private program or service proposed by the parent or the school. If so, that program or service should be examined in light of the current assessment to ensure that assessment results and findings support the goals, objectives, and strategies of the private program.

2. Parent Records

As a member of an IEP team considering the issue of reimbursement, the parent can be expected to have documentation that is essential to the team's deliberations. If the parent, rather than the public school, is proposing the private services, the parent usually will have researched and obtained information about one or more private programs. Even if the public school's representatives on the IEP team are confident about the appropriateness of the public school program, the IEP team still should obtain and consider parent information about proposed private programs or services in order to put all relevant evidence before the team and assure the parent a full consideration of the request.

3. Teacher Records

Teacher logs, notes, and other physical records are necessary for the team to determine whether the public school has provided, or can provide in the future, an appropriate program for the child. The classroom teacher's records help the team establish first whether the IEP was, or can be, implemented and, second, whether the child made or is likely to make progress in accordance with his or her potential as affected by the disability.

4. Scheduled Evaluative Data

Records created and maintained by the school in order to comply with IEP evaluation requirements, whether this consists of teacher data, standardized test data, behavioral data, psychological assessment records, or data from some other source, supply additional evidence about the student's progress or lack of progress in the public school's program. Evaluative data required by the student's IEP should be maintained and preserved for use by the IEP team, and failure to do so may constitute a procedural error. In any event, the failure to maintain evaluative data effectively prevents the IEP team from monitoring student progress and making the essential determination of whether the public school, as opposed to a private program, has provided and can continue to provide appropriate education.

5. School Health Records

Public schools are not required by federal law to reimburse medical treatment (as opposed to medical evaluation) from a private medical provider, nor are they typically authorized to do so by state law. Thus, it is exceedingly rare for a decision maker to require a public school to reimburse private medical services. Nevertheless, medical records may be important in evaluating the student's status, and changes in the student's condition over time, and thus should be examined for that reason alone. School nurses often log important data that is relevant to the student's progress, such as the occurrence of symptoms that might reflect stress from an overly challenging placement, or attempts to avoid certain classes or activities by feigning symptoms. Conversely, genuine medical illness, first noted by the school nurse, may be the cause of a student's failure to behave or respond appropriately and fully to classroom instruction. The school nurse may be the first school employee to note signs that the student is experiencing problems in the community, such as abuse, drug experimentation or behavioral health problems. All these data bear on the issue, in a reimbursement case, of the appropriateness of public school services.

6. Related Service Records

If the student is eligible for special education and has been receiving related services, it is not unusual for disputes to arise over the nature, or quality, of related services that the school has provided or proposes to provide. In such instances, parents may request reimbursement of related services from a private provider on the grounds that the public school's related services are inappropriate and ineffective. Alternatively, it may be argued that flaws in the public school's delivery of related services have impaired or will impair the child's ability to benefit from special education, or mainstreaming, and therefore private school placement is necessary for that reason. The IEP team that considers a reimbursement claim should examine related service records, logs of service delivery, and evaluative information created and maintained by the related service provider. This is necessary both to determine whether currently scheduled related services have been provided as scheduled and to gauge the effectiveness of the related service including its impact on the child's special education. The related service provider's participation on the IEP team should be arranged through either attending the IEP team meeting in person or providing necessary information to the team, including the parent, in some form, prior to the meeting and for discussion at the meeting.

7. Records Concerning the Proposed Private Placement or Service

In a situation where the public school is convinced that private services are necessary to deliver FAPE, and the parent disagrees, it will be essential to study the private program or service in detail in order to determine whether it is both necessary and appropriate. The IEP team should look for problematic circumstances, such as those mentioned earlier, from special education cases where proponents of private programs have failed to justify their appropriateness. There is no sense going to the mat over public school reimbursement of a private program or service that cannot itself withstand scrutiny in a due process hearing.

In a situation where the parent is proposing the private program or service, the IEP team should investigate the proposed program, including obtaining additional information about the program's philosophy, methodologies, decision-making processes, and methods of evaluating student progress. Even if the IEP team is in disagreement over the public school's IEP or services, it may still be necessary to afford this information a fair hearing. And, as a practical matter, uncovering inadequacies or inappropriateness of the private program at this stage may pretermit the dispute, allowing the team to revisit the public school's IEP. Critical information about the private program should include staff qualifications, costs, and any assessment data that has been produced or collected by the private program on the child whose IEP is in question, that tends to justify the need for that program.

If it turns out that the public school's program is or will be appropriate, at least this inquiry has stimulated the team to think creatively about options for the child. If, however, the public school's program is questionable, this research can help the IEP team come to terms with options for private services including the strengths and weaknesses of the specific private program alternative proposed by the parent.

III. WHO SHOULD BE PRESENT AT THE IEP TEAM MEETING TO CONSIDER REIMBURSEMENT, AND WHY?

1. The Parent

Disputes concerning reimbursement of private services almost always pit the parent's wishes against the school's attempts to provide FAPE. Either the school is proposing a private placement that the parent opposes, or the parent is demanding reimbursement claiming that the school has not done its job. In either case the school and parent will hopefully maintain open communication before the team meeting to help frame the dispute for consideration by the IEP team. The parent, of course, must be present or otherwise have input during the team meeting unless very unusual circumstances preclude this.

2. The Child's Special Education Teacher

If the child is eligible for special education and has been receiving services, the child's special education teacher can supply information about the child's daily functioning and progress in school, and the extent of implementation of the IEP and modifications to the general education setting and curriculum. The special education teacher's input and documentation is thus essential to establish two essential facts: whether the IEP has been implemented in special education and whether the child is making progress. If the child is unable to make progress, even in a special education setting or mainstream setting with extensive aids and services, the special education teacher's input will be necessary to establish the specifics indicating the need for private placement.

3. The Child's General Education Teacher

The general education teacher's job will be to help the team explore the appropriateness of the IEP placement and schedule of services for the mainstreamed child. The general education teacher documents the implementation, as well as the success or failure, of supplementary aids and services including modifications. The general education teacher brings documentation and other evidence such as personal anecdotes to illustrate the child's progress or lack of progress in that teacher's classroom. Ordinarily a mainstreamed child who is failing in the mainstream setting will be afforded the chance to reverse his or her failure through the assistance of additional supplementary aids and services, content mastery, or special education services for example in a resource classroom setting, before private placement is considered.

4. A School Administrator

An administrator or designee must participate in every IEP meeting. The campus administrator is responsible for allocating school district resources and, in this capacity, must participate with other IEP team members in determining the most efficient and effective means to deliver services necessary for the student to receive an appropriate education. The administrator's participation assures other team members that the school district stands behind the IEP and will deliver services. The participation of an administrator or designee with substantial authority ordinarily will be necessary to the success of an IEP meeting to consider private placement because of the nature of the issues involved. If it turns out that private services are agreed upon by the team, it should never be necessary for the team to need "higher" approval for its decision.

5. Assessment Specialists and Other Experts

The assessment specialist or related-service expert is the IEP team member having formal training and background to describe what the assessment says about the nature and implications of the child's disability. The assessment specialist thus is the appropriate person to interpret assessment findings in areas requiring specific expertise. A request for private services that rely on a particular instructional methodology or strategy requires discussion of detailed specifics regarding the child's disability. This discussion must address both appropriate instructional methodology and appropriate assessment methods to evaluate the child's present performance and progress in domains affected by the disability. For this reason, the assessment specialist or other expert with relevant training and background, for example an educational appraisal specialist, dyslexia or learning disability specialist, speech/language pathologist, psychologist, or other qualified specialist, should be recruited to assist in determining whether the child requires the private service for an educational reason or whether school-based services alone are appropriate for the child. In general, a person must be present at the IEP team meeting who can interpret any assessment results that are relevant to the team's deliberations.

6. Representatives of the Private Program or Service Provider

It has already been noted that a parent has the right to bring along any representative the parent wishes to an IEP team meeting, and this would include a representative of a private program or service provider. However, the school may wish to invite the representative to the IEP team meeting that considers reimbursement, for several reasons. Having the representative in attendance allows the team to give more of a full and fair hearing to the reimbursement issue. The representative may indeed have valuable input at the meeting, even to the point of aiding public school officials on the team in designing an appropriate program - particularly where the representative is a licensed professional with independent ethical duties to the child. The representative may help the IEP team to clarify and highlight differences of opinion regarding appropriate IEP services and placement. And the other team members may call upon the representative to explain how the private program or service will operate to benefit the child, if the public school program cannot.

IV. THE ORDER OF BUSINESS FOR IEP TEAM MEMBERS

1. The Chairperson

The chair of the IEP team to consider proposed reimbursement for private services should be a person acquainted with the child and family, knowledgeable regarding the child's disability, and familiar with the circumstances leading up to the proposal for private services. The chair must be competent with respect to using IDEA procedural safeguards and able to run a meeting effectively. Because the IEP meeting to consider reimbursement of private services may involve points of serious disagreement and strong emotions, the chair should be someone who can maintain focus on building a record of objective data or evidence to support the IEP team's ultimate decision.

2. The Opening

Once participants have been introduced, the chair of the IEP meeting should begin by summarizing the purpose of the meeting, which is to determine the appropriateness of the IEP and the school's implementation of the IEP, and to consider the appropriateness of placement alternatives proposed by team members. The chair should then review the proposed order of presentations, including the parent and/or the parent's representatives as well as the school district's representatives. The chair should inquire if the parent is satisfied with the notice received concerning the timing and content of the meeting, understands the order of business and the items for decision, and has any request to alter the agenda, raise additional issues for consideration, or present additional matter to the team. If the chair fails to so inquire, the parent and other team members should raise questions and/or additional matters at this opening stage of the meeting.

3. Discussing Assessment Information and Present Performance

The first item of business is to discuss current assessment. The appropriate team member should review the current assessment and eligibility briefly. If new assessment is brought before the team by the parent or the school, that information must be discussed at greater length, along with the recommendations of that assessment for IEP services and placement. If there is disagreement among the team regarding assessment, that disagreement should be discussed until the team has a clear understanding of the specific items or areas of disagreement about assessment and has made a record of same. If there is disagreement, the team should discuss whether further assessment is needed and, if so, what action should be taken with respect to the IEP and placement during the pendency of that assessment.

Following the discussion of assessment, the child's teachers should lead a review of the child's educational goals and objectives, including both special education objectives and any objectives from the regular curriculum that the mainstreamed child is working on. For children with behavioral disabilities, this discussion must include behavior IEP objectives and problem behaviors that are the subject of any individualized behavior management plan or behavior-oriented modifications. Teachers further must review the progress, if any, that the child has made on scheduled objectives and present any documentation they have to establish that the child is or is not making progress. Teachers should present anecdotal information regarding the child's behavior and learning to illustrate why the child is or is not making progress.

Solid evaluative data from the classroom teacher will be essential to establish whether or not the child is making progress as expected. If the school, for example, is proposing the private placement, the teacher or teachers should have data that establishes specific learning and/or behavior problems, as well as reasons why those problems can-not be addressed satisfactorily in a public school setting with the available range of special education and other services. If the school proposes to keep the child in the public school, the teacher will have the first hand information to establish that the child is making progress and that the public school's program is meeting the child's needs.

4. Discussing Special Education
and Related Services

Once the child's disability characteristics, strengths, deficits, and recent learning characteristics and progress have been discussed, the team should explore services necessary for the child to make progress consistent with his or her disability and estimated learning potential. The relevant characteristics of each particular service should be discussed and specified in detail, including the general qualifications of staff needed to implement the service, the amount of service needed for the service to be effective, and the setting or settings where the service is appropriately implemented. If a member of the team wishes to discuss instructional methodology, the team should have a clear understanding of the issues appropriate for discussion on that topic. As presented elsewhere in this volume, methodology ordinarily is an issue only when a team member proposes that the child can receive FAPE only through the use of a particular methodology. Therefore, the team's discussion should focus on examining evidence, if any, tending to establish that a particular method would be *necessary* for educational benefit.

In cases where public school reimbursement of past or current private services is at issue because of alleged IEP deficiencies, the team at some point must determine whether the classroom teacher knew and understood the child's IEP. The team must determine if the IEP was actually and fully implemented in the classroom. The team should *never* take it for granted that the child's teacher knows and understands the IEP or is implementing the IEP fully. If a classroom teacher cannot be present at the IEP meeting, someone from special education must obtain evaluative records regarding IEP implementation from every teacher who works with the child. If a disagreement develops into a due process hearing, a lawyer undoubtedly will do this.

5. Discussing Placement Including Supplementary Aids and Services

It will be particularly important in a reimbursement case for the team to consider and document evidence regarding what is appropriate mainstreaming for the child, including modifications and other aids and services, before discussing the issue of private services. This is true particularly where a team member has proposed private school placement or residential placement. Ordinarily, private placements are chosen because of advertised expertise in working with disabled students. However, this means that the private placement may serve only disabled students and thus may not afford the child opportunities to interact with non-disabled peers in an educational setting. Thus, the team's conclusions regarding appropriate mainstreaming may bear directly on the appropriateness of a proposed private placement.

Once the team has discussed the amount of mainstreaming that would be appropriate for the child, the team must explore the private placement proposal by reviewing all of the information and debating the issues outlined in the preceding paragraphs. Again, the central issues will involve specifics of why it is that the public school cannot offer an appropriate education for the child in the LRE and why the proposed private program or service can.

V. KEY DELIBERATIONS TO DOCUMENT

Any point that is worth serious discussion by the IEP team deserves mention in the written minutes of the team's deliberations. This is particularly true if the point is disputed or may be the subject of an appeal. If the team's decisions are questioned in a due process hearing, the written record can help to establish what the team discussed in the meeting even if the members later become unavailable or cannot remember what took place. In reimbursement situations, the IEP team will want to ensure an unambiguous record of several essential points. (1) Do members agree, or disagree, with respect to current assessment findings and recommendations? If not, then which specific findings and recommendations are agreed upon and which are not? (2) Is further assessment necessary? If so, what kind of assessment, how will it be done, and when? When will the team next convene to consider the results? (3) If members have rejected certain recommendations of the current assessment but are not recommending further assessment, what are the specific reasons for rejecting certain recommendations and accepting others? (4) Once assessment issues are resolved (or specifically framed for appeal), what services, recommended in the assessment, is the public school prepared to deliver? Why does the team believe, or not believe, that those services will provide FAPE? (5) What specific deficits in the public school's program are identified as necessitating private placement or services? Why can those deficits not be remediated in the public school setting? (6) What are the characteristics of the proposed private program or service that make it reasonably likely for the child to benefit? Are the private services fully individualized? Are they any different in nature from what the public school offers? Are they delivered by adequately trained staff? Are staff numbers adequate for the number and characteristics of students? Does the private program evaluate student progress in ways that are generally accepted in the professional community? How often do they evaluate, and what results will be provided to the public school for monitoring purposes? (7) What mainstreaming does the private program provide during instructional time? What noninstructional opportunities exist for the child to interact with non-disabled peers? If the private program does not provide mainstreaming opportunities, is it really true that the child's special instructional needs are so pressing that the team must override LRE considerations? Why, in this case, is LRE of secondary importance?

VI. INVOKING STOP-GAP MEASURES

As with any other type of IEP dispute, the team may recess the meeting to consider reimbursement of private services at any point the team feels further assessment is needed, or additional documentation or references need to be reviewed, or outside persons need to be consulted or perhaps invited to be part of the team, or merely because tensions need time to wind down. Often, a recess, possibly coupled with informal alternative dispute resolution, allows the team members who are in disagreement to find alternatives that will resolve the impasse with an acceptable and appropriate resolution.

INDEX